Schöningh

Discover ...

TOPICS FOR ADVANCED LEARNERS

edited by Engelbert Thaler

Australia and New Zealand

Neither Down nor Under

by Rainer H. Berthelmann

Sprachliche Betreuung: Simone Duxbury-Ziemer

www.schoeningh-schulbuch.de
Schöningh Verlag, Jühenplatz 1–3, 33098 Paderborn

Druck 5 4 3 2 1 / Jahr 2013 12 11 10
Die letzte Zahl bezeichnet das Jahr dieses Druckes.

Umschlaggestaltung: Franz-Josef Domke, Hannover
Umschlagfotos: © WILDLIFE/M. Harvey (l.); © picture-alliance/Bildagentur Huber (r.)
Druck und Bindung: westermann druck GmbH, Braunschweig

ISBN 978-3-14-040104-3

Contents

Australia

The dog-ears in this book give you some useful additional information.

New Zealand

AUSTRALIA

Getting started

- The pictures on this double page show scenes which are typical of Australia. Describe or guess what the people are doing. Which of the pictures arouses your particular interest? Why? Discuss.

Australia – My First Encounter

Number Plates of Australian Vehicles

Activities

Stereotypes

1. Which stereotypes do you connect with 'Oz'? Do you think that, after you have looked at Australia more closely, your stereotypes will dissolve? Give reasons.

Number plates

2. The eight number plates stand for Australia's states and territories. Find out their names with the help of the map on the next page.

An educated guess

3. Before you read the yellow box below, have a guess:
   - What is the area of Australia?
   - How far away is the continent from Europe?
   - What is Australia's population?
   - What does the continent's name mean?

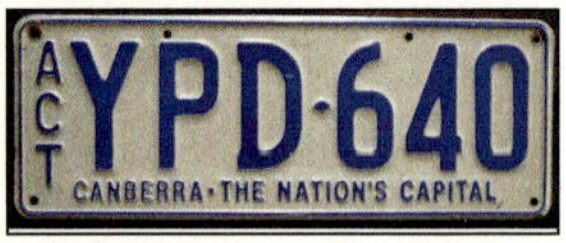

I never knew this about Australia

- The continent's area is 7,686,850 km^2 – a little smaller than that of the United States. The direct distance (i.e. 'as the crow flies') between Berlin and Australia's capital Canberra is about 16,000 km. The actual travel distance, however, is much longer.
- The name 'Australia' comes from 'Terra Australis', which is Latin and means 'southern land'. This name was given to the country by the English explorer Matthew Flinders in 1814.
- In November 2009, the country had an estimated resident population of more than 22 million people. Indigenous people, once the original and the only settlers, now comprise less than 1% of the Australian population.
- Population density: Australians have ca. 350 km^2 per person available. Germany has 231 inhabitants per km^2, or 4.3 m^2 per person. Nevertheless, much of the land in Australia is uninhabitable.
- The Commonwealth of Australia was founded in 1901.

One of Australia's nicknames is 'Oz'.

Maps of Australia

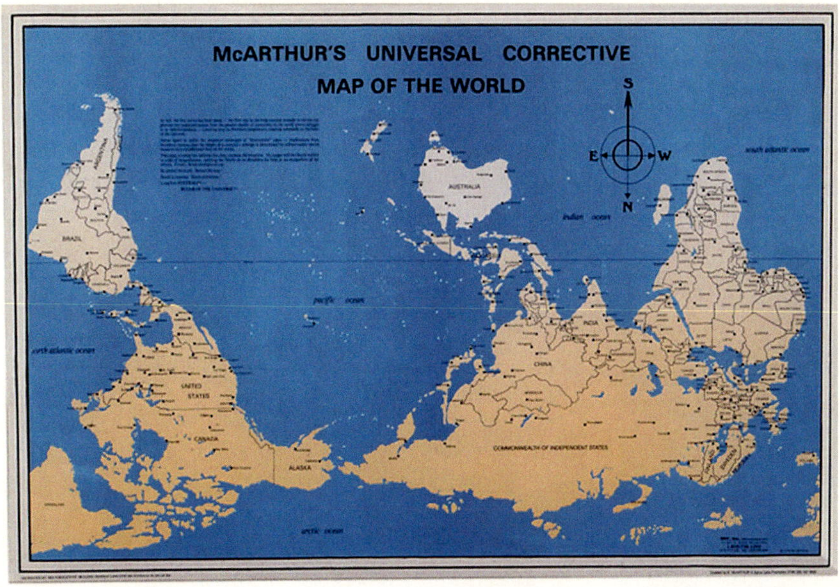

World upside down map

Political map of the Commonwealth of Australia showing the states and territories controlled under a federal government.

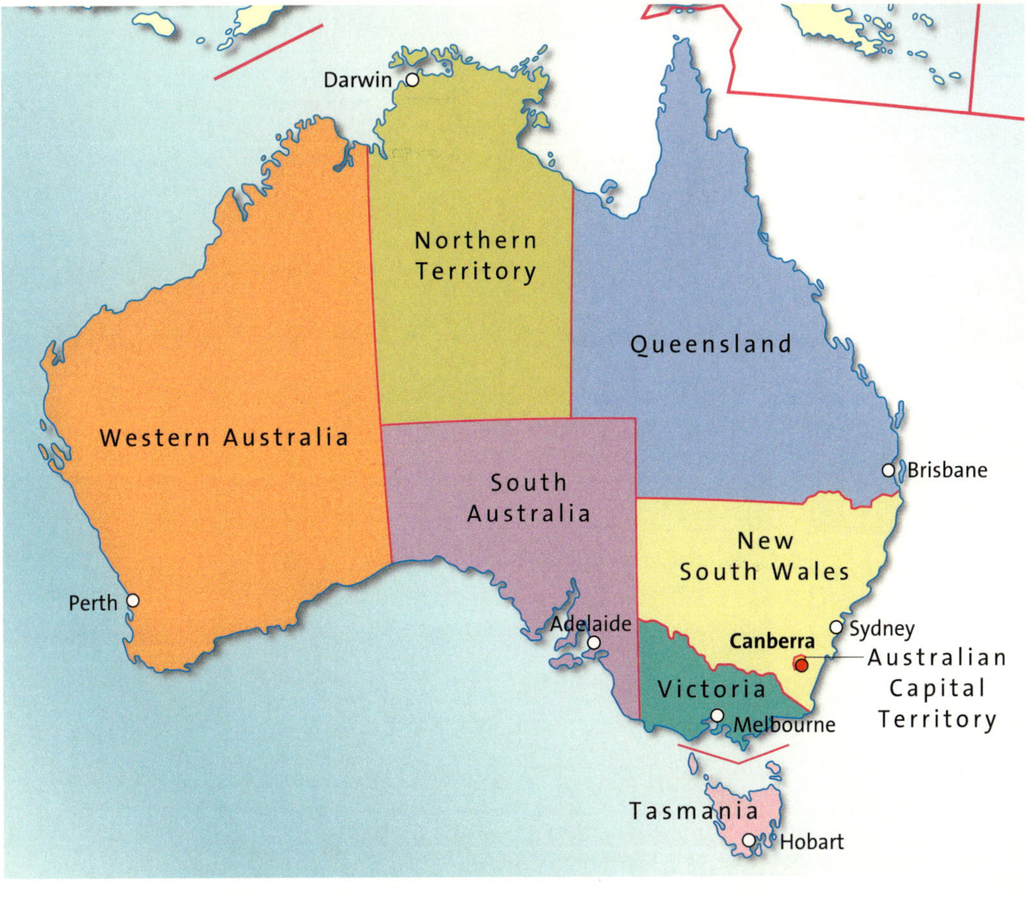

Diverse and Breathtaking Landscapes and Nature

"With diverse and breathtaking landscapes, Australia's natural beauty has captivated Australians and international visitors alike for generations. [...] It is the landscape and geography that has contributed to developing the Australian character and spirit of having a go and pulling together in good times and in adversity."

Australia's Prime Minister Kevin Rudd

Laughing Kookaburra

Sulphur-crested Cockatoo

Ibis

Emu

Blue Mountains, New South Wales

Farmland, Victoria

Eucalyptus wood, Victoria

Daintree Rainforest, Queensland

Outback desert, Northern Territory

Great Barrier Reef, Queensland

Activities

1. Make a fact sheet of what you already know about Australia. Keep this record until you have finished the Australia course. Later, you can compare your knowledge about Down Under before and after you have completed this course.

Comprehension

2. An easy way of keeping track of all your Australia reading and research is to keep a log book. This can be, for example, a 'Down Under Folder'. As you read this book and surf the Internet for information about Australia, write down facts and ideas to remember. As far as possible, collect photos and illustrations as well.

Keeping a log book

3. Page 7 shows two maps of Australia. The upper one has been created with south facing up. Stuart McArthur of Melbourne is said to have drawn it in 1973, at the age of 15, as an exchange student in Japan. He was sick of being taunted by his fellow students for coming 'from the bottom of the world'. Discuss this statement.
The other map is a regular political map showing the states and territories of the Commonwealth of Australia with their capitals.
Complete these tasks:
   a) Count the number of states and territories of the Commonwealth.
   b) First, speculate why the states and territories might have been given the names they have. Then search the web for exact information.
   c) Discuss some of the reasons why Australians might produce and sell such funny upside-down maps of 'Oz' and the world.
   d) Locate the areas represented by the eight number plates shown on page 8.

Discussing maps

4. Brainstorm what the constituent parts of Australia's national flag and of its coat of arms (shown on p. 8) might mean. Prepare and give a five-minute talk about Australia and its national symbols.

Giving a talk

5. Search the web for some of the great men and women who attained fame and honour in Australia. Find out what they are famous for and give a short talk about each of them: Abel Tasman, James Cook, Arthur Phillip, Matthew Flinders, Lachlan Macquarie, John Macarthur, John McDouall Stuart, Harold Lasseter, Ludwig Leichhardt, Brettena Smyth.

Searching the web for great Aussies

6. Describe the landscape pictures on page 10. Then continue the Prime Minister's statement. Give at least three examples in which you try to prove that the geography has indeed "contributed to developing the Australian character".

Discussing the message of pictures

Young People in Australia

National Youth Week

G'day, mates! Have you ever heard of **National Youth Week***? NYW has been running as a national event since 2000. It is Australia's largest festival involving thousands of children and young people all across the country in April every year.*

What is NYW all about?
It aims to encourage young people to:
- share ideas,
- attend live events or showcase their talents,
- have their voices heard on issues of concern to them,
- celebrate their contribution to the community,
- take part in competitions, and have fun!

Who is involved[1]?
High schools, universities and TAFEs[2] take part in the celebrations. Other organisations also get involved in NYW, such as community and youth organisations, official events organisers, sponsors, businesses, Australian, State, Territory and Local Governments.

What happens during NYW?
No matter where you live or what you are interested in, there are plenty[3] of opportunities for you to become involved in NYW, such as: sporting activities, dance parties, community projects, conferences, debates, exhibitions, festivals, forums, live performances.

Competition details

RockIT (Sponsored by Allan's Music)
The theme: Write and record an original piece no longer than 5 minutes that incorporates[4] the theme 'Make a Move'.
Industry Award Prize: a $ 5,000[5] Allan's Music voucher

DesignIT (Sponsored by The Source)
The theme: Create a digital static design that incorporates the theme 'Make a Move'.
Industry Award Prize: a $ 5,000 computer package

SnapIT (Sponsored by Scouts Australia[6] and Ted's Cameras)
The theme: Snap a photo that incorporates the theme 'Action and adventure in the outdoors'. Entries that have been digitally manipulated will not be accepted.
Industry Award Prize: a $ 5,000 photography pack

---

[1]**to involve** *here* to ask or allow sb. to take part in sth. [2]**TAFE** [teɪf] short for **T**echnical **a**nd **F**urther **E**ducation college [3]**plenty** many, a lot [4]**to incorporate** to make sb. or sth. part of something [5]**$** *here always* Australian dollars [6]**Scouts Australia** an organisation for young people that teaches them practical skills (see www.scouts.com.au)

More Australian English:
G'day (hello),
mate (friend, guy).

ShootIT (Sponsored by Commonwealth Bank Foundation and Ted's Cameras)
The theme: Lose the L plates[7] when it comes to money – making smart financial decisions. Figuring out how to use your money wisely can be tricky. It's important to equip yourself with the appropriate advice to make sure you make the most of your money. Shoot a two and a half minute short film about what can happen in a young person's life when they are smart with their money.
Industry Award Prize: a $ 5,000 cinematography pack

WriteIT (Sponsored by Beyond Blue)
The theme: Look for signs of depression, listen to your friends' experiences, talk about what's going on and seek[8] help together. Using these messages about improving mental health as a theme, compose a piece of creative writing in the format of a short film script, short story or poem of no more than 1,500 words.
Industry Award Prize: a $ 5,000 computer package

---

[7]**lose the L plates** refers to 'Learner' plates on the car; *here* take control of yourself and be confident [8]**to seek** to try to get sth.

I never knew this about Australia

- Young Australian of the Year 2007 was awarded to Tania Major, an Aboriginal girl. Since then Tania has become a role model not only for Indigenous youth, but also for all young Australians. The Young Australian of the Year Award recognises those aged 16 to 30 who are outstanding and exceptional young Australians.

Activities

1. Which competitions does National Youth Week comprise? What are their potential participants invited to create? — *Checking comprehension*
2. If you had the chance to take part in NYW, which of the competitions would you take part in? Give reasons for your decision. — *Giving reasons*
3. Do similar competitions exist in Germany? Would you like to have them in your area, too? Discuss. — *Discussing ideas*
4. Make five posters that might attract young people's interest. Give your posters eye-catching headlines, such as 'Get involved', 'Be in the running for cool prizes', or 'Be creative'. — *Making posters*
5. Find out more about Tania Major, and why she has become a role model for young Australians, and about Ms Jonty Bush, the award winner for 2009. Who is the current Young Australian of the Year? — *Searching the web*
6. Imagine German local authorities want you to inform them about NYW. Mediate the text. You need not translate literally into German. — *Mediating*

Celebrate Being a Young Australian

NYW is a joint Australian, State, Territory and Local Government initiative. Ministers for youth all across Australia support NYW. Read one of the 2008 Ministers' Messages concerning the national talent competitions and take a first look at some of the labels and institutions of the NYW's 2009 sponsors and partners shown on this page.

Kate Ellis – Australian Government Minister for Youth

"The Australian Government is pleased to be a part of the ninth annual National Youth Week, celebrating the contribution and value of all young Australians to their local communities. National Youth Week is an opportunity for you to get out there in your community and get involved to make the most out of the celebrations and activities that will be taking place all across Australia between Saturday, 5 April and Sunday, 13 April 2008. 'Shout. Share. Live. Unite.' is this year's slogan for National Youth Week, chosen by young people. This is an open invitation to get involved and celebrate the achievements of young people."

National Youth Week 2009

An Australian, State, Territory and Local Government Initiative

NYW 2008 in review

The week kicked off with a free concert at Martin Place put on by Video Hits. Over 3,000 young people rocked up to see The Presets, Operator Please, Delta Goodrem and Brian McFadden perform. It was broadcast live on Video Hits to around 1.2 million viewers around the country. This was followed by a huge week-long celebration of youth. All up, over 289,470 young people participated in more than 1,645 NYW events. Hundreds of young people around the country proved just how talented they are. We received 532 entries into the National Talent Competition and 3,646 entries into the Win Free Stuff competition. Check out the 2008 NTC and WfS winners.

Imparja

Proudly supporting beyondblue the national depression initiative www.beyondblue.org.au

spress

Look at some of the 2009 sponsors

AFP AUSTRALIAN FEDERAL POLICE

ten

SBS

ACTNOW.COM.AU

Australian Government
Australian Sports Commission

... and partners of NYW.

Talent Comps – 2008 Winners

Read some details from the biography of four of the 2008 winners.

RockIT Senior

Nikki Malvar is an eighteen-year-old journalism student at the University of Technology, Sydney. She has lived in the Philippines, Thailand, the United States and Australia. She enjoys writing and performing music, creating short films, writing pieces of prose, as well as the occasional mathematics. As a result, she currently has a crisis of occupational aspiration[1].

The winning poster by Rhiana Chan

ShootIT Junior

Mark Sebastian has had a passion for comedy since he was able to talk. Maybe even before. Mark started making videos for the popular homevideo-sharing site youtube.com in April 2007, and has already worked up a following, recently being announced as the 11th most viewed Australian comedian on YouTube. With a cult following, Mark Sebastian is destined[2] for stardom. Or at the very least, hopefully not ending up homeless.

DesignIT Junior

Rhiana Chan: There's no time like the present. I am a student from Canberra, currently in Year 10 at Melba-Copland Secondary School. I love all things art and in the past few years I have extended my interest in digital illustration and design. Most of my artwork focuses on people and compositions. I hope to one day be a graphic designer.

SnapIT Junior

My name is Tom Stanford and I live in a small coastal town in Victoria's southwest. I enjoy snapping varying degrees of talent in our local community from bands to skaters. I'm currently in year 11 and hope to be a professional photographer when I leave school.

The winning photo by Tom Stanford

---

[1]**aspiration** ambition, a strong desire to have or achieve sth. [2]**destined** seeming certain to happen or become

Activities

Searching the web and giving talks

1. Work in pairs.
   a) Choose one of the labels of the NYW sponsors and partners on p. 14, and then surf the Internet for more information about it. What do the labels tell you about Australia? Give a short talk on your topic.
   b) Search the web for information about the bands and singers mentioned on p. 14. Introduce them to the class.

Comparing

2. What hopes and plans for the future do the four young Aussies have? Are they similar to yours? Draw up mindmaps and compare.

Discussing the point of view

3. Two of the short biographies are told in the first person, the other two in the third person. Are there any differences as to their effectiveness? Which perspective do you like more? Why? Discuss.

'Aussie' ['ɒzi] is a popular short form for Australian.

Sydney – Capital of the Young

Sydney is one of the most beautiful cities in Australia and the world. Describing the pictures, make a guess as to what young people in Sydney might be able to do as a job or in their free time.

From top left to bottom right: The Strand Arcade; Sydney Opera House; Central Business District; The Domain; Diving at Manly Beach; Luna Park

News around Australia

"Australians can't bear it that the outside world pays so little attention to them, and I don't blame them. This is a country where interesting things happen, and all the time." (Bill Bryson: *Down Under*. Black Swan. Sydney 2001) The following extracts from Australian newspapers reflect different aspects of everyday life Down Under. Read them, and then do the tasks given on page 23.

(1) Immigration and Australian values

A land where all kids can play

by Ahmed Fahour

The social inclusion we enjoy in this country today is surely the envy[1] of the world. I think of my own experience. My parents journeyed here from Lebanon a little under 40 years ago. They had no English and little money. We lived in the northern suburbs. The community was working class; Turks lived alongside Maltese; Lebs alongside Italians; Yugoslavs alongside the Greeks. It was really only at university that I began to appreciate[2] the opportunities opening up for me. I had no problem in being accepted – just another working-class wog[3] with a strong work ethic. Never for a moment did I think of myself as excluded from the normal relationships and activities available to the majority of people, be they economic, social, cultural or political. This is a wonderful Australian achievement.

[1]**envy** wish that you had sb. else's possessions, abilities, etc. [2]**to appreciate** *here* to understand how useful sth. is [3]**wog** *infml. here* offensive term for dark-skinned immigrant, esp. Greek, Italian, Lebanese, etc.

(2) IT in Australia

Slaying[1] the hackers

by Penelope Debelle

At Maroochydore on Queensland's Sunshine Coast in 2000, the shire council[2] experienced what it thought were teething problems[3] with a new wastewater system. Radio commands to wastewater pumping stations were disappearing, pumps were failing and alarms meant to alert[4] staff to faults were not going off. By monitoring every signal that passed through

Reading
Bill Bryson's book about Australia is a must!

the system, the Maroochy Shire Council discovered that someone was hacking into its system and wreaking havoc[5]. The hacker was Vitek Boden, a disgruntled[6] former employee who had lost his job and wanted revenge [...]. The University of South Australia in Adelaide is emerging as an international leader in a project to protect urban infrastructure from hackers. Headed by the director of the UniSA[7] Forensic Computing Lab, Dr Jill Slay, the project has been given $ 60,000 under the Department of the Prime Minister and Cabinet's Research Support for Counter-Terrorism program and will collaborate with Commonwealth agencies in developing a protection model for SCADA[8] systems.

[1]**to slay** to kill sb., *here* to defeat [2]**shire council** local government [3]**teething problems** troublesome difficulties in the initial stages of a new project [4]**to alert** to warn [5]**to wreak havoc** to cause a lot of problems [6]**disgruntled** annoyed, disappointed [7]**UniSA** **Uni**versity of **S**outh **A**ustralia [8]**SCADA** **s**upervisory **c**ontrol **a**nd **d**ata **a**cquisition

(3) Sports

The day the city came out to say thanks

by Andrew Prentice

Sydney. Olympians Malcolm Page, Lachlan Renshaw and Iain Murray joined their Australian teammates for a triumphant homecoming parade in George St in the CBD[1] yesterday. Flanked by the likes[2] of Libby Trickett and gold medal pole vaulter[3] Steve Hooker, the trio were greeted by thousands of adoring[4] fans who turned out to celebrate the achievements of the athletes in Beijing. It was a real carnival atmosphere with marching bands, life-size bouncing kangaroos, green and gold confetti and raucous[5] cheering. Page, who won gold with fellow northern beaches resident Nathan Wilmot in sailing's 470 tandem class, was blown away[6] by the level of support. "To have so many people come out and cheer us on is fantastic," he said. Renshaw echoed those sentiments. "Any time you have patriotic supporters waving flags and cheering you on makes you proud to be an Australian," he said.

[1]**CBD** **C**entral **B**usiness **D**istrict [2]**the like** someone similar [3]**pole vaulter** *Stabhochspringer* [4]**adoring** loving someone and feeling proud of them [5]**raucous** very loud, noisy [6]**to be blown away** to feel very surprised

(4) Living in a megacity

You don't have to live in Melbourne

by Mike Rawlinson

Bernard Salt talks of the future shock of "mega Melbourne" with a population in 2051 of 6.5 or 8 million ("Future shock of mega Melbourne", September 29). He omitted to ask whether we want Melbourne to grow at this rate, or canvass[1] whether we can do anything about it. Melbourne urgently requires an infrastructure "catch-up". But its rate of population growth could be slowed by policies that increase the relative attractiveness of Victoria's regional cities as places to live, work, raise families and retire. In the information age, there are many occupations that are not tied to capital cities. Taking all factors into account[2], why live in Melbourne if a better quality of life was available in, say, Warrnambool[3]? It's up to us to tell government what we want.

Cook's Cottage, the childhood home of James Cook, was shipped from England to Melbourne in 1934.

Street scene in Melbourne

[1]**to canvass** *here* to talk about a problem [2]**to take into account** to consider facts and details when making a decision [3]**Warrnambool** beautiful and prospering coastal town on the Great Ocean Road in Victoria

Ur kid's L8 4 skool – Schools go hi-tech
by Miawling Lam

Schools are following the lead of tech-savvy[1] students by text messaging their parents when they fail to show up to class. Parents are also receiving emailed updates about their child and schools are setting up digital noticeboards and television screens around their grounds. Federation of Parents and Citizens' Associations of NSW spokeswoman Sharon Johnson said such initiatives offered great comfort to guardians. "It's a way we can be involved instantly and it's usually very versatile[2] and efficient," she said. Cumberland High School, in northwest Sydney, set up an SMS system last term to alert parents of unexplained absences. Principal Terry Wilson said since its introduction last term absenteeism had fallen by three per cent.

(5) IT in school

Postgraduate Education – All abroad
by Andrew Stevenson

Being a student for the first time, living in a city away from home: it's a dream for many young people, even if there are nightmarish[3] moments along the way. Before Carrie Collins could make her move to Sydney from British Columbia, Canada, there was her husband to persuade, a house to rent out and a car to sell. Now head-down, tail-up in a demanding master's of speech language pathology at the University of Sydney, Collins has had no trouble adjusting[4] to her new surroundings. "I'm exploring Sydney every chance I get. I'm looking forward to my vacation, when I can explore more of Australia."

(6) Studying and living in Australia

Their goes you're grammar
by Karen Collier

VCE[5] students have such a poor grasp[6] of English that one university is offering remedial classes[7]. Melbourne academic Baden Eunson said more than half of his first-year students struggled with proper punctuation and sentence expression, and almost all failed to identify nouns or adjectives. He believes disturbing numbers of pupils are passing VCE despite a poor grasp of English, because of "trendy" teaching and computer spell-checks masking problems. Recruitment companies, too, complain of receiving resumes riddled with errors. Adecco said more than half of all submitted resumes contained spelling, punctuation or grammatical mistakes. The words "there" and "their" were commonly misused, as were "to" and "too" and "your" and "you're".

(7) Education deficit

Can you find the mistake in the picture above?

---

[1]**savvy** clever [2]**versatile** able to be used in many different ways [3]**nightmarish** very frightening [4]**to adjust** to become familiar with a new situation [5]**VCE V**ictorian **C**ertificate of **E**ducation [6]**grasp** ability to understand sth. [7]**remedial class** special course for students with learning difficulties

Cathy Freeman supports the Commonwealth Games Education Program

Boxing as a free time activity

Sydney Harbour Bridge

Taking a break: schoolchildren in Sydney

I never knew this about Australia

- About one million migrants arrived in each of the six decades following 1950.
- Australian values include: respect for the freedom and dignity[1] of the individual, equality of men and women, freedom of religion, commitment to the rule of law, parliamentary democracy, a spirit of egalitarianism that embraces[2] mutual respect[3], tolerance, fair play and compassion for those in need, pursuit of the public good, and equality of opportunity for individuals, regardless of their race, religion or ethnic background.
- In 2008, there were 459,692 enrolments[4] by full-fee paying international students in Australia on a student visa, nearly one-third of them – or 142,000 – were enrolled in vocational[5] education.
- The various climates allow a wide range of sporting activities all year around: rugby, surfing, golf, cricket, horse racing, cycling, tennis, swimming, winter sports, etc. *"Aussie, Aussie, Aussie, oy, oy, oy!"* is a cheer or chant often heard at Australian sport events.
- Catherine Freeman has been the first Indigenous woman who won a gold medal for Australia during the Sydney 2000 Olympics. During the Beijing 2008 Olympic Games Australian athletes won 14 gold medals.
- Sydney's population is expected to grow from more than four to six million by 2035. Melbourne has a population of 3.7 million (2008). Between 2001 and 2006 figures show that 7,000 people came to live in Melbourne's CBD every year. The average age of residents in Melbourne's inner reaches[6] was 25, compared with 37 across Australia.
- Australian school takes a modern approach to exams. For example, students at a Sydney girls' school are now being encouraged to take their phones, laptops and MP3s into exams and even phone a friend if they want help with a question.

---

[1]**dignity** the sense of your own value and importance [2]**to embrace** *here* to willingly include [3]**mutual respect** respect for each other [4]**enrolment** the process of arranging to join a school, university, course, etc. [5]**vocational** related to a specific occupation or profession [6]**inner reaches** inner-city districts

Activities

1. What do these texts tell you about Australia? Give a summary of each of them. In your summaries, include the information given in the box on p. 22.

Giving a summary

2. Search the web addresses provided or surf other sites for further details about the issues dealt with in texts 1 to 7, and then present and discuss the topics.

Using the Internet

   1) Ahmed Fahour describes his and his parents' good experiences as immigrants to Australia. How might immigrants to Germany sum up their feelings? (www.immi.gov.au/media/fact-sheets)
   2) What do you learn from this text about Australia's scientific skills? (www.anu.edu.au/discoveranu/content/podcasts/itc_industry)
   3) The third article is about Sydney's triumphant welcome for Australian Olympians. Australian athletes rank top five in the world. In which disciplines? Which sports stars do you know? (www.athletics.com.au, www.paralympic.org.au)
   4) Does Bernard Salt want to live in a city of six million or more residents? Would you? Discuss some of the pros and cons of living in a megacity. (http://tingurl.com/m52wht)
   5) Search the web for more information about IT in Australia's schools and compare it to your school. (http://tinyurl.com/lktg9c)
   6) Andrew Stevenson writes about a Canadian woman who moved to Australia to study and work there. Can you imagine studying Down Under? (http://studyinaustralia.gov.au)
   7) Do German students have similar problems with their native language? What is the VCE equivalent to in Germany? (https://aei.gov.au/AEI/CEP/Australia/EducationSystem/default.htm)

3. Search newspapers like 'The Age', 'The Australian' or 'The Sunday Telegraph' for more everyday events in Australia. You might simply decide to read any article you are interested in, or choose a particular topic of interest you want to look at more closely.

Reading newspapers on the net

4. Which song is the official national anthem of the Commonwealth of Australia? Find an audio version of Australia's anthem on the Internet, and listen to it. First, read and translate the lyrics, and then discuss the message of the song.

Listening to Australia's national anthem

5. Another very popular national song is "I am Australian", written by Bruce Woodley and Dobe Newton in 1987. It was, for example, sung during the Australian National Mourning[1] Service for the victims of the 2009 Black Saturday[2] bush fires. Search the web for the lyrics of this song and discuss why it might have become so dear to the 'Aussies'.

Exploring another popular song of the Australians

---

to mourn to feel very sad [2]**Black Saturday** On Saturday, 7 February, 2009, devastating bushfires that were burning across Victoria killed more than 200 people, badly damaging many villages and towns and leaving more than 7,000 people homeless.

Australian Culture

Aboriginal signs are painted on stones along the roads in Alice Springs.

Australia's culture has developed over hundreds and thousands of years with contributions from the Aboriginals, British convicts and settlers and immigrants from many other nations.
Along with language, religion, music, craft, architecture, cuisine, poetry, paintings, fashion photography, movies, there are many more expressions of culture Down Under that have come to be seen today as 'Australian'.
On the following pages, you can learn about the culture of Australia and about Australian artists, musicians, writers and actors.

Aboriginal Art

You can find references to Aboriginal art in many places – be it on litter bins (above) or at the airport (below).

Harry Tjutjuna started painting only in the last few months of 2005. He is in his late seventies; it remains difficult to verify[1] the year of his birth. He has a grown family and is twice a widower. Harry is a senior law man and *ngankari*, a traditional healer. He came in to Ernabella[2] as a young person and was educated at the Ernabella mission school. As a young adult, he took an active part in the life of the newly settled community, working on bore sinking[3], fencing, gardening, and with the sheep which the mission ran to pay its way and provide the medical services and education which were the purpose of the mission's foundation in 1937. Harry concentrates on a few important subjects in his paintings: kangaroo men and (marsupial[4]) mouse women – two of the significant totemic[5] Creation beings of his country; and men thinking about (chasing) women, i.e. finding their life partners; and women thinking about (and running away from!) men, i.e. considering their suitors; and young girls playing *milpatjunanyi*, the traditional way of telling stories in the sand[7]. He also often paints the *Kungkarangkalpa* (seven sisters) story, from a very male perspective. He is one of the greatest characters at the art centre with a wonderful sense of humour and big laugh!

[1]**to verify** to state that sth. is true [2]**Ernabella** a small Aboriginal community in the south of the Outback [3]**bore sinking** making waterholes [4]**marsupial** an animal which carries its babies in a pocket of skin on its body, e.g. kangaroos and koalas [5]**totemic** referring to a totem, i.e. an animal, plant, etc. that is thought to have a special spiritual meaning [6]**Creation** the act by Aboriginal spirits of making the world and everything in it [7]**to tell stories in the sand** to draw pictures in the sand while telling the story behind them

Activities

1. What subjects do artists like Harry Tjutjuna concentrate on?
2. Describe the examples of Aboriginal art which can be found everywhere in Australia. What are their characteristic features?
3. Search the web for more information about Aboriginal art. Prepare a multimedia presentation on this issue.

Aboriginal Music

Yothu Yindi

Yothu Yindi, pronounced as "yo-thoo yin-dee", is the name of a famous Australian band and translates as "child and mother". Their unique style combined the sounds and instrumentation of western rock 'n' roll with songs and performances that date back tens of thousands of years. They took the ancient song cycles of north-east Arnhem Land[1] – featuring such traditional instruments as the *bilma* (ironwood clapsticks) and *yidaki* (didgeridoos) – and juxtaposed[2] them with western pop sounds to present a true musical meeting of two diverse cultures. They also took traditional Yolngu dance performances – describing the behaviour of crocodiles, wallabies[3], brolga[4] and other fauna of their homelands – and worked them into the context of contemporary performance.

The result is a band that's been called "the most powerful blend of indigenous and modern music to emerge from the world music scene". Coming together in 1986, Yothu Yindi consists of both Yolngu (Aboriginal) and Balanda (non-Aboriginal) musicians and embodies[5] a sharing of cultures.

The band recorded their first album *Homeland Movement* in Australia's bicentennial year[6], 1988. Yothu Yindi performed bicentennial protest concerts in Sydney, headlined the first Festival of Aboriginal Rock Music in Darwin (later appearing in the television documentary *Sing Loud Play Strong*) and embarked[7] on a 32-date tour of the United States and Canada with Australia's most politicised rockers Midnight Oil. Also that year, the band's founding member and lead singer, Mandawuy Yunupingu became the first Aboriginal person from Arnhem Land to gain a tertiary degree[8] when he graduated with a Bachelor of Arts (Education) from Deakin University[9].

Bilma

Yidaki

[1]**Arnhem Land** a Northern Territory region as large as Portugal, home to the Indigenous Yolngu people [2]**to juxtapose** to put together [3]**wallaby** a small kangaroo [4]**brolga** a tall and slender cranelike bird that has mythological meaning for Indigenous people [5]**to embody** *here* to include [6]**bicentennial year** marking 200 years since the first British settlement in Australia in 1788 [7]**to embark** *here* to start [8]**tertiary degree** university degree (gained at an education level following the secondary education level in high school) [9]**Deakin University** a university in Melbourne, Victoria

Activities

1. What kind of music does Yothu Yindi produce? What instruments do its members play? — Comprehension

2. Go to www.yothuyindi.com. Close your eyes and listen to Yothu Yindi's music. What visions come to your mind? Discuss. — Discussing visions

3. Read between the lines. What does the last paragraph of the text tell you about the band's political activity, and what do you conclude from this about the place of indigenous people in Australian society? — Reading between the lines

Waltzing Matilda

A. B. "Banjo" Paterson

Before you read

$10 banknote featuring A. B. "Banjo" Paterson

Billabong in the MacDonnell Ranges

The famous bush ballad "Waltzing Matilda" is Australia's unofficial national anthem. Read this short extract from then Prime Minister Paul Keating's address at the celebrations on 6 April 1995 for the 100th anniversary of the first performance of the song: "Waltzing Matilda was born in a drought era, of course, and it is not hard to imagine that this might have had some effect on the melancholy theme of the song. And there is equally no doubt that in all the varieties of hard times Waltzing Matilda has galvanised[1] the spirit of countless Australians. If culture is that which defines a people, if it is the expression of their collective sentiment, Waltzing Matilda sits at the centre of our culture – it's a well spring[2] of the national sentiment, a pool, a billabong."

Once a jolly *wandering shearer* camped by a *waterhole,*
Under the shade of a *kind of eucalyptus* tree.
And he sang as he watched and waited till his *tin can* boiled
'Who'll come a-waltzing Matilda with me?'

Chorus: Waltzing Matilda, waltzing Matilda,
You'll come a-waltzing Matilda with me.

Down came a *sheep* to drink at the *waterhole.*
Up jumped the *wandering shearer* and grabbed him with *joy*
And he sang as he put that *sheep* in his *bag for keeping food in*
'You'll come a-waltzing Matilda with me!' – Chorus

Up came the *owner of the sheep station* riding on his *horse.*
Up came the *soldiers of lower rank,* one, two, three.
'Whose is that jolly *sheep* you've got in your *bag for keeping food in*?
You'll come a-waltzing Matilda with me!' – Chorus

Up jumped the *wandering shearer* and sprang into the *waterhole.*
'You'll never catch me alive!' said he.
And his ghost may be heard as you pass by that *waterhole,*
'Who'll come a-waltzing Matilda with me?' – Chorus

---

[1]**to galvanise** *here* to stimulate into action [2]**well spring** a place where water comes up from a deep hole in the ground

Activities

1. Read and translate the song, then look for it on www.youtube.com and listen to it. While listening, substitute the original words for the words and phrases printed in small letters.
2. Learn the new words and retell the song in your own words.

More Aussie slang:
roo (kangaroo),
joey (baby kangaroo),
brumby (wild horse).

Brett Whiteley – One of Australia's Avant-Garde Artists

Brett Whiteley

Brett Whiteley is one of Australia's most revered[1] artists. His works hang in many galleries, including the National Gallery of Australia in Canberra, the Tate Gallery in London and the Museum of Modern Art in New York. Whiteley was born 1939 in Sydney, New South Wales, and grew up in Longueville, a harbourside suburb in North Sydney. By the age of seven, he had won his first art competition. He was sent to boarding school[2] at Scots College, Bathurst, and in 1956, was awarded first prize in the Young Painters section of the Bathurst Show. He left school mid-year and took night classes in drawing at the Julian Ashton Art School in Sydney while holding down a job at an advertising agency. In 1960, aged 21, Whiteley left Australia on a Travelling Art Scholarship[3], and by 1961, had settled in London. In London, he met many other painters, including fellow Australians Arthur Boyd and John Passmore. His reputation grew worldwide with his success in winning the international prize at the second Biennale de Paris (International Biennial for Young Artists) in 1962. Whiteley's acclaim[4] continued to grow throughout the seventies and eighties. In the last years of his life, Whiteley travelled far and wide, taking in England, Bali, Tokyo, and spending two months in Paris. On 15 June 1992, he was found dead from a heroin overdose in a motel room in Thirroul on the NSW coast. He was 53 years old.

Brett Whiteley, *Almost once*, 1968/1991, Art Gallery of NSW. This monument stands in The Domain, one of Sydney's most popular parks.

[1]**revered** respected and admired [2]**boarding school** a school where the students live as well as study [3]**scholarship** an amount of money that is given to sb. by an educational organisation to help pay for their education [4]**acclaim** *here* reputation

Activities

1. Describe Whiteley's work "Almost once". Try to interpret it. — Describing art
2. Imagine you are visiting Sydney. Write an email to a German friend of yours in which you tell him or her about Brett Whiteley and what you think was especially fascinating about him. — Mediating
3. Search the web for more information about the other artists mentioned in the text: Arthur Boyd and John Passmore. — Searching the web

Finnikin of the Rock

Melina Marchetta

Melina Marchetta

This is the beginning of "Finnikin of the Rock" (2008), a mystical story of homeland and identity by the best-selling Australian author Melina Marchetta. The author lives in Sydney. Her novels have been published in more than 14 countries and 11 languages. Her first book "Looking for Alibrandi" was also published in Germany.

When it finally appeared in the distance, Finnikin wondered if it was some phantom half-imagined in this soulless kingdom at the end of the world. There had always been talk that this land had been forsaken[1] by the gods. Yet perched[2] at the top of a rocky outcrop, cloaked[3] in blue-grey mist, was proof to the contrary: the cloister[4] of the Goddess Lagrami.
From where they stood, the flat expanse that led to its fortified entrance resembled[5] the softness of sand over a desert. Finnikin could see a trail of pilgrims with their heads bent low, each with a sack across their shoulder and a staff[6] in their hand. They made a line across the low-lying country like tiny insignificant ants at the mercy[7] of the nothingness surrounding them.
'We must hurry,' the King's First Man urged, speaking the Sarnak language. Sir Topher had decided that once they reached this wasteland of Sendecane they would use the language of the neighbouring kingdom to the north. At the inn, two nights before, he had made it known that they were pilgrims themselves: holy men who had come to the end of the earth to pay homage[8] at the greatest temple of the blessed Goddess Lagrami. To be anything else in this part of the land would raise suspicion and fear, and Finnikin had come to realise that those full of fear were the most dangerous of people.
As they drew closer to the rock, the terrain beneath[9] their feet began to change. What Finnikin had thought was sand turned out to be a thick clay-like[10] substance that tested his balance. They were walking on a sea bed, and by nightfall the waters would return and there would be no hope of leaving this place until the next low tide.

---

[1]**to forsake** to leave and give up [2]**perched** located on top or on the edge of sth. [3]**cloaked** hidden, covered [4]**cloister** *Kreuzgang* [5]**to resemble** to be similar to sb. or sth. [6]**staff** *here* stick [7]**at the mercy of** entirely in the power of, helpless [8]**to pay homage** to show respect for sb. [9]**beneath** under(neath) [10]**clay** a type of heavy sticky earth that can be used for making bricks, pots, etc.

Activities

Retelling a story

1. Read the text. Then retell the beginning of the story in your own words. Concentrate on the situation, plot and characters of the story.

Continuing a story

2. Guess how the story could go on. Discuss.

Thinking up a story

3. Write down the possible structure of the whole narrative on one page: introduction, main part, conclusion. Then compare your ideas.

Searching the web

4. Find out more about the author. Who is she? What does she write?

Australia

Baz Luhrmann

Nicole Kidman and Brandon Walters in "Australia"

Australian studios have produced many films that have gained international acclaim. Cinema-goers around the world have seen such films as "Crocodile Dundee", "Looking for Alibrandi", "Rabbit-Proof Fence", or "Babe, the Gallant Pig". One of the most recent Australian blockbusters is Baz Luhrmann's film "Australia" starring Oscar winning actress Nicole Kidman and Hugh Jackman.

"Australia", released[1] 2008/2009 and set between 1939 and 1942, is the story of Lady Sarah Ashley (Nicole Kidman), an English, aristocratic woman, who leaves England to follow her husband to Australia. Tragically, her husband is murdered shortly before she arrives. Therefore, Lady Ashley finds herself inheriting a cattle station the size of Belgium in north Australia. In order to save it, she and a rough-hewn[2] cattle drover[3], simply called 'Drover' (Hugh Jackman) must undertake a long cattle drive to Darwin. Drover, a white man, is friendly with the Aborigines. It is revealed[4] that he had previously married an Aboriginal woman, but she had died after being refused medical treatment in a local hospital because of her race.
Lady Sarah is captivated[5] by the young, half-Aboriginal boy Nullah (Brandon Walters). Nullah is drawn to perform a ceremonial coming-of-age walkabout with his Indigenous grandfather "King George", but is instead captured[6] by the authorities and sent to live on Mission Island together with many more half-Aboriginal children. This was possible back then as part of the policy of forcibly removing Aboriginal and Torres Strait Islander (Indigenous) children from their families, especially those of mixed race. Later, these children became known as the Stolen Generations.
Drover leads a team of six riders, including Lady Sarah, Drover's Aboriginal brother-in-law Magarri (David Ngoombujarra) and Nullah, to drive the 1,500 cattle to Darwin. In the course of that journey, Lady Ashley falls in love with Drover. A few months after arriving in Darwin, they are caught in the Japanese bombing of northern Australia during World War II, but in the course of this, Nullah and the other children are rescued from Mission Island[7].

---

[1]**to release** *here* to make a film available for people to see or buy [2]**rough-hewn** *here* lacking good manners [3]**drover** sb. who moves cattle from one place to another [4]**to reveal** to make known sth. that was secret or unknown [5]**to captivate** to attract sb. [6]**to capture** to catch [7]**Mission Island** fictitious place in the north of Australia

Activities

1. Describe the main characters starring in the film. To what extent do they reflect Australian history?

   Describing people

2. What is meant by the term "Stolen Generations"? Search the web to find out more about this issue.

   Searching the web

3. Do you know any of the above-mentioned titles or perhaps another famous Australian film? Choose a film and tell your classmates about it.

   Retelling a film

Don't miss out on seeing the film "Australia"!

***'Neighbours Night'* poster**

"Neighbours" – An Australian TV Soap

"Neighbours" began with Danny Ramsay having a terrible nightmare[1] about his brother, Shane, being injured whilst diving[2]. The next morning, Julie Robinson leaves Number 26 to go and spend some time with her friend Lorraine, the girl who is due to marry her boss Des Clarke the following morning.

Still running today, this is how one of Australia's most seen soap operas started in 1985. Similar to German "Gute Zeiten, schlechte Zeiten", the series follows the daily lives of several families who live in the six houses at the end of Ramsay Street. The storylines explore the romances, family problems, domestic squabbles[3], and other key life events affecting the various residents.

Read how "Neighbours" stars and fans reacted to the shocking and devastating bushfires in Victoria in February 2009 (also see annotation about Black Saturday on p. 23).

Neighbours fans and stars alike joined forces this week in the biggest event in *Neighbours Night*[4] history to raise[5] money for Victoria's Bushfire victims. Over 20 actors from the show – past and present – volunteered their time on 16th February to meet the fans, who paid to attend the one-off[6] event. The evening raised a total of $31,105.50, which is being donated to the Red Cross Victorian Bushfire Appeal Fund. [...] The *Neighbours* production team kindly donated signed *Neighbours* memorabilia[7], which were auctioned off throughout the evening. Also auctioned on the night were contributions from tour operators and accommodation providers throughout Melbourne.

Kylie Minogue, the most famous *Neighbours* actress ever

George Josevski, Managing Director of Bunyip Tours and the official *Neighbours Night*, was gobsmacked[8] by the generosity[9] of everyone involved.

"Never have I experienced anything like this since I started the *Neighbours Nights* back in 1998, and I am humbled[10] by the generosity of the actors, fans, and everyone who volunteered their time to make this evening a night to remember."

Throughout the night, *Neighbours* fans were entertained by Sam Clarke (Ringo) who sang with his band The Keepers, as well as Steve Bastoni (Steve Parker), Blair McDonough (Stu), Ben Nicholas (Stingray), Patrick Harvey (Connor) and Stefan Dennis (Paul Robinson), who all sang with resident[11] *Neighbours Night* band 'Waiting Room', fronted by Alan Fletcher (Dr Karl).

---

[1]**nightmare** a very frightening dream or experience [2]**to dive** *here* to jump into water from a height [3]**squabble** argument [4]**Neighbours Night** event carried out on a regular basis in Melbourne, where fans can meet stars from the show [5]**to raise** *here* to collect [6]**one-off** happening only once [7]**memorabilia** things that you keep or collect to remember a famous person, event, or time [8]**gobsmacked** very surprised, shocked [9]**generosity** willingness to give money, spend time, etc. in order to help people, give pleasure, etc. [10]**humbled** *überwältigt* [11]**resident** (adj.) *here* fixed, regular

Activities

1. What event do "Neighbours" fans celebrate once a week in Australia? Describe what goes on at these events.

Comprehension

2. Who usually profits from these events? Analyse the reasons why they are organised. Think about this question carefully, then discuss your answers.

Analysing a commercial strategy

3. Do you know of similar events or other advertising strategies in Germany? If so, tell your classmates about them.

Describing strategies

4. "GZSZ" is not on the tube yet in Australia. Imagine you are publicity consultants who have been given the task to make this series popular Down Under. In groups of four to five, think up potential strategies. Finally, introduce your ideas to the class and decide which strategies would probably be most effective.

Mediating

5. Why not celebrate Australia Day (on 26 January) by having an Australia Party in your class? There is not much you need to do:
   - First, decide when and where you want to have your party and which guests you want to invite.
   - The party should be well prepared. For example, you can make Australia-related events the central theme of your party. Work in pairs or groups. Some might talk about Brett Whiteley, and present examples of his art. Others might read extracts from the books by Melina Marchetta or another Australian writer. A third group could prepare a PowerPoint presentation of famous sights of Australia, etc. You could also tell each other about Australian films or soaps you have seen or read about.
   - You could also arrange an Australian barbecue party.
   - Be creative! Think up other interesting events.

Celebrating Australia Day

Australian postcard by Bruce, Sheila and the Endangered Species Gang

NB: Aussies love having a 'barbie' (barbecue) and singing songs.

Multicultural Australia

What Place Multiculturalism?

Peter Jensen

Before you read

Peter Jensen

"One of the greatest strengths of our nation is our cultural diversity. The Government is committed to Multicultural Australia, with policies and programs that unite us as Australians working to advance Australia fair[1]." Decide whether this key statement of Government multicultural policy is confirmed in the following extract from an essay by Dr Peter Jensen, Archbishop of Sydney. Discuss.

[...] I think multiculturalism may be a word that has now gone beyond its usefulness, because it has also been taken to mean that we have no culture, that there is nothing basic here in Australia which we can identify as our culture. And if that is the meaning of what is said, then we will not have the resources to face the challenges[2] that lie before us in the next two decades. We are going to have to go back to cultural roots, in order to be able to face those challenges. And I would like to say in other words, there is an Australian culture, it's no longer British, it may have been 50 years ago, it's no longer British, it's now Australian, but there are elements of it from our past which still shape us and which we need to be aware of.

When I think of Australia, sitting as I do here in Sydney, and I realise this is not true of Australia as a whole, and I think of the Australian face, I think of a Chinese face. And when I think about Church – I am member of the Anglican Church, the old Church of England – if my church in the next 50 years is not Chinese and Korean and Greek and Italian, then it won't survive, and yet all of these people will be speaking English. Our language is one of the most significant cultural features about us. We'll be speaking Australian English, discernibly[3] Australian English, but we will be speaking one language, we won't be speaking many languages. Language not only enables us to relate, of course, but it also carries with it the freight[4] of history and of understanding of the world. That's why multiculturalism can never actually be the final word on our society. Our society is a united society, united by this single language, and all it carries with it, and united therefore in the capacity[5] for us to relate to each other but enor-

Chinatown in Sydney

---

[1]**advance Australia fair** the name and last line of the chorus of Australia's national anthem; cited from: *Multicultural Australia: United in Diversity*. Updating the 1999 New Agenda for Multicultural Australia: Strategic directions for 2003 – 2006, © Commonwealth of Australia [2]**challenge** sth. that tests strength, skill, or ability [3]**discernibly** sth. that can clearly be recognised [4]**freight** load, *here* problematic issues [5]**capacity** *here* ability

mously enriched – Australia has been and will be enormously enriched – by the migrants who have come here with all their traditions and their history and their understanding of the world as well. We're certainly not going to be the English living Down Under.

Far and Near

Ouyang Yu

in australia
i am as far from any australians
as china is from australia

and i am as near them
as a cloud
near the sky

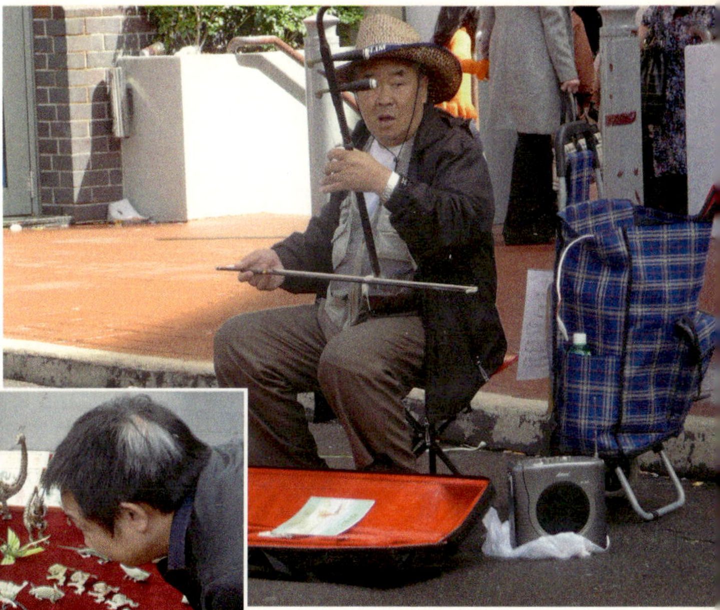

Fiddler in Sydney's Chinatown

Chinese craftsman and street vendor in Melbourne

Pakistani men waiting for the City Circle Tram in Melbourne

I never knew this about Australia

- Australia has welcomed settlers and new citizens from more than 200 countries. They have brought their languages and cultures with them and successfully combined ethnic and cultural diversity with national unity.
- In 2006, there were 4.4 million first generation Australians (24 % of the population). First generation Australians are people living in Australia who were born overseas.
- Second generation Australians are Australian-born people living in Australia, with at least one overseas-born parent. In 2006, there were 3.6 million second generation Australians (20 % of the population).
- Third-plus generation Australians are Australian-born people whose parents were both born in Australia. In 2006, there were 10.1 million third-plus generation Australians (56 % of the population).
- In every census[1], most Australians have reported an affiliation[2] with Christianity. In 2006, this majority was 12.7 million people. However, affiliation to Christianity had fallen from 96 % in 1911 to 64 % in 2006. The ongoing growth in arrivals from Asia has resulted in large increases in the number of Buddhists, Muslims, and Hindus. In 2006, these three faiths[3] collectively accounted for 907,000 affiliates compared to 468,000 a decade earlier in 1996.

---

[1]**census** an official process of counting a country's population and finding out further details about its people [2]**affiliation** the connection or involvement that sb. or sth. has with a political, religious, etc. organisation [3]**faith** *here* belief and trust in God

Activities

Summing up

1. Sum up how Peter Jensen sees multiculturalism in Australia.

Discussing cultural diversity

2. Today, people of all faiths are welcome in Australia. Which future for religious life does Jensen foresee for his country? What do you learn from the text about multiculturalism in Australia? Discuss.

Giving opinions

3. Explain what your idea of ethnical multiculturalism is.

Writing an article

4. Imagine you are asked to write an article on immigration to Germany for your partner school. Collect information: How many immigrants are there in Germany? When did they come? Where do they come from? What problems do they have? etc.

Two mottos
of Australian policy:
Migrate Oz! Go Matilda!

Neighbours

Tim Winton

People in Australia: He is from China.

He is from New Zealand, she is from Lithuania.

He is from France, she is from Germany.

When they first moved in, the young couple were wary[1] of the neighbourhood. The street was full of European migrants. It made the newly-weds[2] feel like sojourners[3] in a foreign land. Next door on the left lived a Macedonian family. On the right, a widower from Poland.

The newly-weds' house was small, but its high ceilings and paned windows gave it the feel of an elegant cottage. From his study window, the young man could see out over the rooftops and used-car yards the Moreton Bay[4] figs[5] in the park where they walked their dog. The neighbours seemed cautious about the dog, a docile[6], moulting[7] collie.

The young man and woman had lived all their lives in the expansive outer suburbs where good neighbours were seldom seen and never heard. The sounds of spitting and washing and daybreak watering came as a shock. The Macedonian family shouted, ranted[8], screamed. It took six months for the newcomers to comprehend the fact that their neighbours were not murdering each other, merely talking. The old Polish man spent most of his day hammering nails into wood only to pull them out again. His yard was stacked with salvaged[9] lumber. He added to it, but he did not build with it.

Relations were uncomfortable for many months. The Macedonians raised eyebrows at the late hour at which the newcomers rose in the mornings. The young man sensed their disapproval at his staying home to write his thesis[10] while his wife worked. He watched in disgust as the little boy next door urinated in the street. He once saw him spraying the car from the back step. The child's head was shaved regularly, he assumed, in order to make his hair grow thick. The little boy stood at the fence with only his cobalt eyes showing; it made the young man nervous.

---

[1]**wary** careful because of possible danger or harm [2]**newly-wed** someone who married a short time ago [3]**sojourner** sb. who stays in a place that is not originally their home
[4]**Moreton Bay** a large bay on the eastern coast of Australia, not far from Brisbane
[5]**fig** *Feigenbaum* [6]**docile** quiet and easily controlled [7]**to moult** to lose feathers or hair [8]**to rant** to talk very loudly [9]**to salvage** to save [10]**thesis** a long piece of writing as part of an advanced university degree

Cultural diversity ...

... everywhere ...

... and every age

In the autumn, the young couple cleared rubbish from their back yard and turned and manured[11] the soil under the open and measured gaze of the neighbours. They planted leeks, onions, cabbage, Brussels sprouts and broad beans and this caused the neighbours to come to the fence and offer advice about spacing, hilling, mulching[12]. The young man resented[13] the interference, but he took careful note of what was said. His wife was bold enough to run a hand over the child's stubble and the big woman with black eyes and butcher's arms gave her a bagful of garlic cloves to plant.

Not long after, the young man and woman built a henhouse. The neighbours watched it fall down. The Polish widower slid through the fence uninvited and rebuilt it for them. They could not understand a word he said.

As autumn merged into winter and the vermilion[14] sunsets were followed by sudden, dark dusks[15] touched with the smell of woodsmoke and the sound of roosters crowing[16] day's end, the young couple found themselves smiling back at the neighbours. They offered heads of cabbage and took gifts of grappa and firewood. The young man worked steadily at his thesis on the development of the twentieth century novel. He cooked dinners for his wife and listened to her stories of eccentric patients and hospital incompetence. In the street they no longer walked with their eyes lowered. They felt superior and proud when their parents came to visit and to cast shocked glances[17] across the fence.

In the winter they kept ducks, big, silent muscovies[18] that stood about in the rain growing fat. In the spring the Macedonian family showed them how to slaughter and to pluck[19] and to dress[20]. They all sat around on blocks and upturned buckets[21] and told barely-understood stories – the men butchering, the women plucking, as was demanded. In the haze[22] of down[23] and steam and fractured dialogue, the young man and woman felt intoxicated[24]. The cat toyed with severed heads. The child pulled the cat's tail. The newcomers found themselves shouting.

But they had not planned on a pregnancy. It stunned them to be made parents so early. Their friends did not have children until several years after be-

---

[11]**to manure** use waste matter from animals to improve the soil and help plants grow [12]**mulching** covering the ground with organic substances [13]**to resent** to feel upset or angry [14]**vermilion** very bright red colour [15]**dusk** the time before it gets dark [16]**to crow** to make a loud high sound [17]**to cast a glance** to quickly look at sb. or sth. [18]**muscovy** large duck [19]**to pluck** *here* to pull the feathers off a dead bird [20]**to dress** *here* to clean and prepare meat or fish [21]**bucket** a small open container with a handle [22]**haze** smoke, dust or mist [23]**down** *here* soft fine feathers [24]**intoxicated** drunk, excited

ing married – if at all. The young woman arranged for maternity leave[25]. The young man ploughed on with his thesis on the twentieth century novel.
The Polish widower began to build. In the late spring dawns, he sank posts and poured cement and began to use his wood. The young couple turned in their bed, cursed him behind his back. The young husband, at times, suspected that the widower was deliberately[26] antagonising[27] them. The young wife threw up in the mornings. Hay fever began to wear him down.
Before long the young couple realised the whole neighbourhood knew of the pregnancy. People smiled tirelessly at them. The man in the deli gave her small presents of chocolates and him packets of cigarettes that he stored at home, not being a smoker. In the summer, Italian women began to offer names. Greek women stopped the young woman in the street, pulled her skirt up and felt her belly, telling her it was bound to be a boy. By late summer the woman next door had knitted the baby a suit, complete with booties and beanie[28]. The young woman felt flattered[29], claustrophobic, grateful[30], peeved[31].
By late summer, the Polish widower next door had almost finished his two-car garage. The young man could not believe that a man without a car would do such a thing, and one evening as he was considering making a complaint about the noise, the Polish man came over with barrowfuls[32] of woodscraps[33] for their fire.
Labour came abruptly. The young man abandoned[34] the twentieth century novel for the telephone. His wife began to black the stove[35]. The midwife[36] came and helped her finish the job while he ran about making statements that sounded like queries[37]. His wife hoisted[38] her belly about the house, supervising his movements. Going outside for more wood, he saw, in the last light of the day, the faces at each fence. He counted twelve faces. The Macedonian family waved and called out what sounded like their best wishes. [...]
And then came the pushing[39]. He caressed[40] and stared and tried not to shout. The floor trembled as the young woman bore down in a squat[41]. He felt the power of her, the sophistication[42] of her. She strained[43]. Her face mottled[44]. She kept at it, push after push, assaulting[45] some unseen barrier, until suddenly it was smashed and she was through. It took his wind away[46] to see the look on the baby's face as it was suddenly passed up to the breast. It had one eye on him. It found the nipple. It trailed[47] cord[48] and vernix[49] smears and its mother's own sweat. She gasped and covered the tiny but-

Multicultural school class on a trip

---

[25]**maternity leave** time that a mother is allowed to spend away from work when she has a baby [26]**deliberately** intentionally, planned [27]**to antagonise** to annoy sb. very much [28]**beanie** a small round hat [29]**flattered** pleased [30]**grateful** thankful and happy [31]**peeved** annoyed [32]**barrowful** small box on wheels full of sth. [33]**scrap** leftover material that is no longer used for the purpose it was made for [34]**to abandon** to stop, to give up doing [35]**to black the stove** to polish a stove with black paint [36]**midwife** a specially-trained nurse whose job is to help women when they are having a baby [37]**query** question [38]**to hoist** to raise, to lift [39]**pushing** *here* pressing down to get the baby out [40]**to caress** to stroke someone in a way that shows you love them [41]**to bear down in a squat** *im Hocken gebären* [42]**sophistication** *here* the woman's instinctive knowledge of the subject [43]**to strain** to try very hard [44]**mottled** covered with spots [45]**to assault** to attack [46]**it took his wind away** he was unable to breathe [47]**to trail** to pull sth. behind you [48]**cord** *Nabelschnur* [49]**vernix** the waxy white substance found on the skin of newborn humans

tocks[50] with a hand. A boy, she said. For a second, the child lost the nipple and began to cry. The young man heard shouting outside. He went to the back door. On the Macedonian side of the fence, a small queue of bleary[51] faces looked up, cheering, and the young man began to weep. The twentieth century novel had not prepared him for this. (1,188 words)

[50]**buttocks** the part of your body that you sit on [51]**bleary** unable to see very clearly, because you are tired or have been crying

Activities

Analysing the text

1. Determine what type of text this is. Give reasons and examples to explain why you think so.

Giving a summary

2. Read the text twice. Afterwards, give an oral or written summary of the story in about 100 words.

Commenting on a character

3. Make a grid to show visually how the single characters and their behaviour develop. Comment on this development.

Writing a script and producing a play

4. Work in two groups. One group writes a script based on this story. The other group produces a radio play. Alternatively, the whole class might act out the story as a role-play.

City Welcomes New Citizens

Minister for Immigration and Citizenship, Senator Chris Evans (right), joins new Australian citizens on Citizenship Day at the National Museum in Canberra.

Some came to Australia from Vietnam via Germany and another came from India via the USA. Their stories were diverse but they had a common bond[1] of all wanting to be Australians. The ten people, whose countries of origin included Vietnam, the UK, Sudan and India, were sworn[2] in as Australian citizens by Colac Otway[3] Mayor Chris Smith last week in a special ceremony to celebrate Australian Citizenship Day. The ten were Davina and Daniel Noakes. Andrew Ryan and Linda West, all from the UK, Vi Buu and Anika Dam and Hue Vong and Trung Tran from Vietnam. Manyang Mar from Sudan and Phil Wipple from India. Trung Tran, of Colac, said he had followed his sister and her family to Australia because he was seeking a more challenging life. He said he had a good job working in information technology but decided to emigrate in 2006 because Australia offered a better quality of life and a more challenging life. He works as an IT assistant at Otway Community College in Colac

[1]**bond** sth. that unites two or more people [2]**to swear in** to make sb. promise do behave well and do their best [3]**Colac Otway** a Local Government Area in Victoria; Colac is a city north-west of Melbourne

and hopes to advance his career in IT. Phil Whipple of Apollo Bay was born in India but spent many of his younger years in the United States. He has been in Australia for five years and has an Australian wife and a daughter in school in Australia. Mr. Whipple said he decided to become a citizen of Australia because he loved the country. The ten became Australian citizens on September 17, which has been celebrated as national Citizenship Day since 2001.

Three of the most famous German Australians:
Ludwig Leichhardt
Hans Heysen
Wolf Blass
NB: For the first hundred years of European settlement, Germans were the largest ethnic group on the continent.

Generations in Australia – 2006

	Person	Proportion of population	1st generation Australians	2nd generation Australians	3rd-plus gen. Australians
Ancestry	**in thousands**	%	%	%	%
Australian	7371.8	37.1	1.8	17.3	34.9
English	6283.6	31.6	19.3	21.2	51.6
Irish	1803.7	9.1	12.5	14.0	80.1
Scottish	1501.2	7.6	18.1	20.7	77.3
Italian	852.4	4.3	27.1	42.3	41.2
German	811.5	4.1	18.1	20.4	74.1
Chinese	699.9	3.4	74.2	21.0	16.9
Greek	365.2	1.8	34.4	45.6	23.4
Dutch	310.1	1.6	34.2	44.4	53.6
Indian	234.7	1.2	77.6	20.5	17.5

Source: www.ausstats.abs.gov.au – A Picture of the Nation; shortened

Activities

1. Where did these 'new citizens' come from? What were their reasons for emigrating?

   Comprehension

2. Interpret the table. What migration trends does it reveal?

   Interpreting statistics

3. Find out who L. Leichhardt, H. Heysen and W. Blass were and which part they played in Australian history and society. Write a brief sketch of their lives and display it in your classroom.

   Writing a biographical sketch

Ed Kuepper is a famous Australian rock, punk & blues singer of German descent.

Australia and Me – Interview with Stephen O'Grady

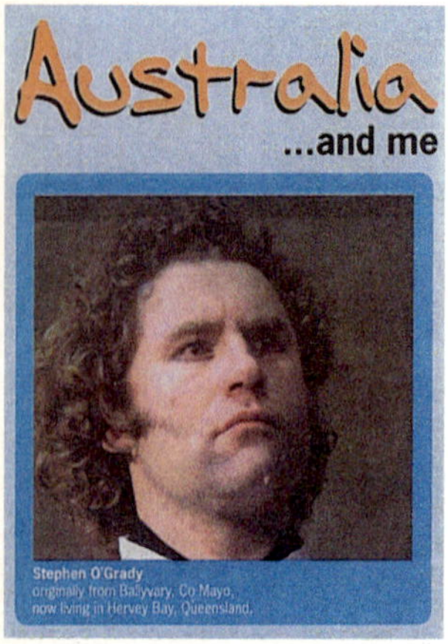

Stephen O'Grady, originally from Ballyvary, Co Mayo, Ireland, now living in Hervey Bay, Queensland

What is your background and how did you wind up coming to Oz?
I had an arts degree and a master in philosophy from UCD[1] before becoming sports editor of Mid West Radio in 1995. In 1997 I left there to become sports editor of the Mayo News and moved to become the paper's new editor in 2004. I arrived in Australia on September 4, 2006 with my partner Cait ...

Describe what you do here.
I'm a journalist with the Fraser Coast Chronicle in Hervey. It's a daily regional paper with a circulation[2] of 10,000 and it's actually owned by Tony O'Reilly. There's not much variation in the work compared to what you would do at home. Councils, police, crime are all regular aspects of a journalists work and they tend to be the same the world over. Working for a daily paper is a different challenge though.

What do you do for fun?
To be honest there's not much time for fun and I don't think we've been able to do as much as we would have liked because we probably became slaves to jobs too quickly. I was involved in a drama group in Hervey Bay[3] and I played the Reverend John Hale in the production of Arthur Miller's *The Crucible*, which was my first time doing anything like that and it was great fun. I also starred in a short film playing a guy[4] who pretended to be Pierce Brosnan, which was very interesting. I really enjoy a few beers at the weekend and watching the NRL[5]. [...]

How often do you go back to Ireland?
I'm going home at Christmas for the first time in two years, three months and 14 days! My father and my brother have been over here though and Cait's nephew was up here with us too.

What has changed about your life since you came to Australia?
Not enough! We probably settled a bit too quickly but I feel I have certainly become a better journalist and because a lot of Aussies don't like the taste of hard work, if you work hard out here, you will progress.

---

[1]**UCD** **U**niversity **C**ollege **D**ublin [2]**circulation** *here* number of copies produced in each edition [3]**Hervey Bay** town on the east coast of Queensland, not far from Fraser Island [4]**guy** *infml.* friend, man [5]**NRL** **N**ational **R**ugby **L**eague

Activities

Comprehension

1. Is Stephen happy and satisfied that he has come to Australia? Give reasons.

Conducting an interview

2. Do you know anyone who came to Germany as a first generation immigrant? Try asking them the questions of this interview. You may also add more questions. Write the answers down.

We Are Australians – Letters from Immigrants (I)

Read two short biographies. They were written by people who came to Australia long ago and have been living in Melbourne ever since.

Anni Radle on the Eureka Tower in Melbourne

I am Anni Radle. My husband, daughter and I left Austria on the 12.07.1958 because of the shortage of housing and landed in so-called sunny Australia. My first shock was we arrived in August when it was winter, we had no warm clothing or blankets, it was freezing. Nevertheless, I was fascinated by the sea and the beautiful clean beaches.
There was plenty of work. When we introduced one of our friends or relatives to work for the company, our boss would give us a cash bonus. Back then we did not have to depend on other countries for our mineral resources, as well as gold, opal, gas, etc. The highlight of my life was when I discovered that there was an Austrian Choir, which I joined immediately. Today, most of the time we are together with people who speak German. *Eines darf man nicht vergessen: Australien ist ein junges Einwanderland mit Multikultur.* There are certain districts where people from different nations *unter sich sein wollen*, for example, the Chinese, Greeks, Italians, Dutch, Germans and others.
We preserve our culture whichever way we can. We are still very loyal to our *National-Feiertag* which we celebrate every year with enthusiasm. We still have a strong dialect though. We still slip in a German word here and there. During Christmas holidays all factories and schools are closed for approximately 4–6 weeks, and almost everybody has a picnic on the beach or by the river.
Every 3–4 years, we return to our mother country to visit our loved ones who we had to leave behind. Even though we have DVDs, videos and TV which keep our home fires burning for our country, every now and then we would hear a song or see a program which gives us *Heimweh*.

Eureka Tower
(Height: 300 m)

German Club celebrating Melbourne Cup Day

We Are Australians – Letters from Immigrants (II)

Bruno Schwaerzler came to Australia from Germany in the sixties. Read his biographical note carefully. What does he say about his feeling of citizenship?

Bruno Schwaerzler and his wife

Young people having a party at Melbourne Convention Centre

In 1960, we were married and had our first child. Due to the shortage of housing in Germany, I could not find a flat in the region of my work. We decided to go to Australia where the climate is warmer and houses are of simple structure, hoping to have our own home one day soon.
The trip to Australia took five weeks by ship. We had 19 hours of English lessons on board. That was the only English we knew. I found work immediately; however, the systems here were quite different. All measurements were English such as inches, feet, yards and miles, Fahrenheit temperatures, ounces and pounds, points and gallons, pennies, shillings and pounds and many more. This has all changed now. We found Australian people most kind, helpful and easy going. People help each other. After four years, we moved into our own home which I had designed myself. To establish a garden was quite easy, neighbours and friends gave me lots of plants and cuttings and they all grew.
Today, Melbourne is a conglomerate of more than 220 nationalities and 115 religious groups, where I feel like a child of the world as we live in wonderful harmony. Most nationalities have their own clubs to keep their own culture alive. Everyone is permitted to visit those clubs. We still sing many hundreds of German *Volkslieder*, read our own history, dance and keep our German festivities. I am not a half-German and half-Australian but a full German and a full Australian. It is great to live here.

Activities

1. How do Anni and Bruno feel about their Australian citizenship?
2. Ask the ten questions the two are seemingly answering in their letters.
3. To what extent do their life stories correspond with the data given in the table "Generations in Australia" on page 39?
4. Do you know any people who came to Germany to live and work? If not, search for famous people who have chosen Germany as their new home. Present what you have learned about them to the class.

Citizenship Testing

The Australian Citizenship Amendment (Citizenship Testing) bill 2007 was introduced into Parliament on 30 May, 2007 and was passed by the Parliament on 12 September, 2007.

The Australian citizenship test plays a valuable[1] role in both encouraging people to find out more about Australia, as well as understanding the responsibilities and privileges being an Australian citizen brings. There is no separate English language test, however you will need a basic understanding of English to pass the test. The test is in English and consists of 20 multiple-choice questions. It includes three mandatory[2] questions based on the responsibilities of Australian citizenship. The test has a pass mark[3] of 60 per cent, including correctly answering all three mandatory questions.

Everything you need to know to pass the test is contained in the free test resource book "Becoming an Australian citizen". It gives migrants to Australia the information they need to better understand what it means to be an Australian. The book covers Australia's values (respect for the equal worth, dignity and freedom of the individual, freedom of speech, freedom of religion and secular government, freedom of association, support for parliamentary democracy and the rule of law, equality of men and women, equality of opportunity, peacefulness, tolerance, mutual respect and compassion for those in need), as well as Australian history, culture and geography, Australia's national symbols and emblems, Australia's parliamentary system of government, and the responsibilities and privileges of being an Australian citizen.

Certificate handed to new citizens together with a memento card displaying the words of the pledge

[1]**valuable** *here* important [2]**mandatory** compulsory, obligatory [3]**pass mark** the percentage of points needed to be successful

Activities

1. Skim all texts of this chapter (pp. 32 to 43) to find out which values are held in high esteem in multicultural Australia.

Skimming texts

2. What feelings do immigrants have when they look back at their coming Down Under and staying there? Discuss.

Discussing feelings

3. This is Australia's Citizenship Pledge:
"From this time forward, under God, I pledge my loyalty to Australia and its People, whose democratic beliefs I share, whose rights and liberties I respect, and whose laws I will uphold and obey."
(A person may choose to make the Pledge with or without the words 'under God'.) Interpret these words. What would keeping this pledge mean to a new citizen of Australia?

Interpreting the citizenship pledge

4. Is there a citizenship test for immigrants who want to become a citizen of Germany? Do new citizens of our country have to take a citizenship pledge, too? Should they have to? Hold a class debate on this topic. Discuss the pros and cons.

Discussing citizenship

Outback but not Back of Bourke

School of the Air

Covering 1,300,000 square kilometres, the School of the Air (SOA) in Central Australia is "the world's largest classroom". It offers a wide range of educational services and activities to isolated primary children in the southern half of the Northern Territory, the extreme north of South Australia and the south-east of Western Australia. On page 48, you can find some additional information on the School of the Air. The following letter was written by Shannon, a year 8 student studying and living in an Adelaide boarding school. Read what the School of the Air meant to her personally.

"On air" lesson in the Alice Springs SOA

Spinifex grass around the cattle station

This is the homestead where Shannon and her parents live.

Back of Bourke is an Australian expression referring to a remote and underdeveloped area.

Erldunda[1], *20 Dec., 2008*

Hi,

My name is Shannon Kilgariff. It's the first days of summer holidays. I'm at home. My parents run a cattle station right in the Red Centre of Australia. From preschool to year 7, I attended ASSOA (Alice Springs School of the Air). This was extremely different in many ways to any other school I later found out when I went to boarding school. One of the huge differences is that it was just my brother and me in the classroom, not a whole class and we were three year levels[2] apart, which made it even more different. My mother taught me at home throughout my time at ASSOA, which is very different to a classroom with a real teacher. The work we had to do was only maths and English in a form called a 'set'. Each set went for 10 days and then we would send the set in to my teachers in Alice Springs and they would then mark it and send it back. This was always so exciting because the teachers always gave us surprises like stickers and small toys for our good work. We had 3 lessons a week on the two-way radio, which was hard because everyone would always try to talk to each other and you couldn't see the teacher. Then the computers came. That was excellent because now we could see the teachers and they controlled who could speak and who couldn't. They gave us demonstrations in art, music, maths and English, which was much better than just the ordinary maths and English. Four times a year, we would go to AS for something called 'in-school', which is when the whole school comes in and we have a week with our teachers and do activities and classes. These were always a lot of fun because we got to meet the other students who we would talk with over the radio or computer. SOA work was not very hard, especially compared to normal school. However, it was not boring, just like normal school. If we ever needed help, our mum would help us or we would have to ring our teachers for their help over the phone. School of the Air is a completely different experience to normal school but it was a good experience to have.

Yours, Shannon

[1]**Erldunda** area situated at the road junction of the Stuart and Lasseter Highways
[2]**level** *here* class, year

I never knew this about Australia

- The first School of the Air was established in Alice Springs in 1951 to provide education for children living in the remote areas of the Outback. At the time, it was the only one of its kind in the world, and high frequency radio was the mode of communication for school lessons. Almost all Schools of the Air now operating in Australia started out by using the Royal Flying Doctor facilities.

Frequently Asked Questions

How many students are on the School of the Air? In 2008, the Alice Springs School of the Air (ASSOA) had 114 students The average number of students over the past 20 years has been 120. Australia-wide, an average of 4,500 students participate in lessons via the SOA system. The school year begins around the end of January and ends in mid-December.

How many grades are taught? Nine levels – from pre-school to year 7, i.e. the students are from four and a half to 12 – 13 years old.

What subjects are taught? Year 7 students participate in lessons that would ordinarily be done in a regular school. Students are also offered some electives such as language and art.

What technology is being used today? In 2003, the school embarked on a major project involving the use of two-way satellite equipment. The implementation of the technology, and development of teaching material and strategies is referred to as IDL (Interactive Distance Learning).

How much time do students spend on PCs? At the higher year levels, teachers are very careful not to have students doing work that requires more than 50 % of their day on PCs.

How much correspondence work is done? Students spend 5 to 6 hours a day working on their lessons at home. The lessons are prepared by teachers at the school and supervised by 'govies' (i.e. governesses – employed tutors) or parents, usually mum.

Do the students only learn at home? No, they have to participate in at least 3 in-school visits a year – usually of one week duration each time.

How many Aboriginal students are there? This varies from year to year. It can vary from a handful to as many as 30, as was the case in 2003.

Alice Springs after a hurricane

Activities

Mediating

1. Write an information leaflet for German-speaking tourists comprising the most important facts about the Alice Springs School of the Air.

Answering a letter

2. Write a personal letter in which you ask Shannon more questions about ASSOA, and tell her about a regular German school.

Royal Flying Doctor Service

The Royal Flying Doctor Service (RFDS) not only provides medical aid[1] in emergencies for the people of the Inland, but also a comprehensive health care and community service. The Service covers more than 7,150,000 sq kms, an area larger than Western Europe, reaching into the very heart of the Australian Continent, the land of the flying doctor, the flight nurse, and pilot.

The world's first air ambulance was founded by John Flynn (1880 – 1951). John Flynn began his work in 1912, at a time when only two doctors served an area of some 300,000 sq kms in Western Australia and 1,500,000 sq kms in the Northern Territory. It did not take him long to realize that air transport and radio were needed to break the isolation of the Red Centre and to provide adequate medical care for its people. But he had to wait many years before he could translate his vision of a flying doctor service into practice.

The Flying Doctor Service, then known as the Aerial Medical Service, became operational on May 15, 1928. The first flying doctor of the Service was Dr K. St. Vincent Welch and the first flying doctor pilot, Arthur Affleck of Qantas. Qantas, today a major international airline, was in those days still a small bush airline, known as the Queensland and Northern Territory Aerial Service (Q.A.N.T.A.S.).

When the Flying Doctor Service first started operating in 1928, there was no radio communication between the base at Clocurry and the outstations[2]. What was needed at the outstations, which could include cattle or sheep stations – huge grazing properties[3], small settlements, mission and police stations – was a cheap and reliable[4] two-way radio[5]. The man who solved the problem of radio communication for the Flying Doctor Service was a young inventive genius, Alfred Traeger from Adelaide. Traeger developed a two-way radio set which he thought would be suitable for the outstations. Initially, the operator had to turn a handle to provide power for the set's generator. Voice transmission was at that stage inefficient and Morse Code had to be used.

In the 1970s, the Service faced a major re-equipment program with the introduction of the single sideband[6] mode of transmission. Since the 1990s, high frequency (HF) radio communication has fallen each year, following the installation of standard telephones in remote areas. Whereas, a few years ago, all calls for medical assistance were received by radio, today this represents only about 2 % of all such calls, the vast majority being made by telephone or satellite telephones. However, there is still the need to protect the small number of people who must, by circumstance, rely on the HF network – e. g. small communities who cannot connect to the standard telephone, mobile users, including exploration camps, Aboriginal outstations, tourists, and simply as a back-up to the standard telephone in remote[7] areas.

"If you start an idea, nothing can stop it."
(John Flynn, 1919)

John Flynn

One of the Morse keys used in the Alice Springs telegraph station

•— ••— ••• — •—• •— •—•• •• •—

This means 'Australia' written in Morse Code.

[1]**aid** help [2]**station** *here* a large farm [3]**grazing property** large farming area where cattle or sheep can eat grass [4]**reliable** sb. or sth. you can trust [5]**two-way radio** a radio that both sends and receives messages [6]**single sideband** a very efficient long-distance voice radio transmission system [7]**remote** far from towns or other places where people live

The famous "School of the Air" also uses the Flying Doctor radio network – however, this also is declining[8] with the advance of other technologies. While the flying doctors could not function without aircraft or communications, they are, by nature of their work, the very cornerstone[9] of the Royal Flying Doctor Service. Their work is also very demanding. There is always a doctor on call to respond to an emergency at any time – day or night. Often the 'inlander' can reach a flying doctor in less time than the average city or suburban dweller[10] can contact his or her doctor by telephone. There is nowhere in the 80 % of Australia covered by the RFDS where a patient cannot be reached within two hours. Emergency flights are made in cases of serious illness or accident when the condition of the patient is serious enough to warrant[11] immediate medical attention and possible evacuation to a hospital. A significant fact is that by far the bulk of the medical aid provided by the Royal Flying Doctor Service of Australia is provided free of charge to those who live, work and travel in Australia's outback.

---

[8] **to decline** to decrease, to go down [9] **cornerstone** sth. that is extremely important [10] **dweller** a person who lives in a particular place [11] **to warrant** *rechtfertigen*

Annual statistics on the RFDS Australia, 2008	
Service area (sq kms)	7,150,000
Patients attended to	105,800
Aerial evacuations	24,000
Healthcare clinics	7,500
Distance flown (kms)	16,000,000
Number of aircraft	42
Bases	20
Bases including a Visitor Centre	10
Staff (incl. part-time)	493

RFDS Radio Communications Centre

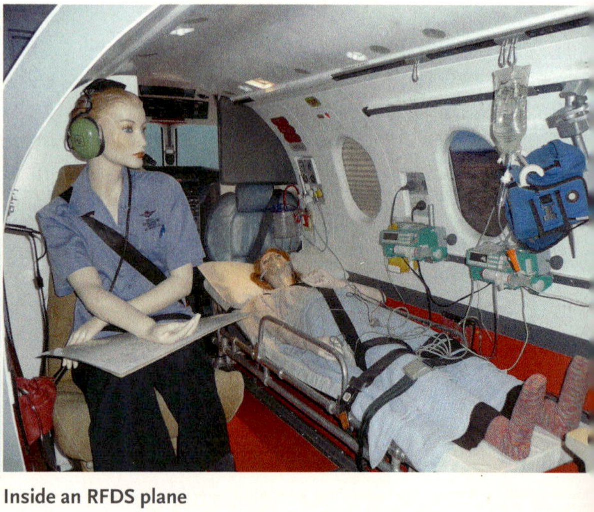
Inside an RFDS plane

Activities

1. Scan the text and the table to find out the answers to these questions: — Scanning a text
   a) When did the RFDS start?
   b) What area does the RFDS cover?
   c) Who was its founder?
   d) What technical equipment was used then, and what is used now?
   e) How many people did the RFDS attend to in 2008?
   f) What did they have to pay for the service?
   g) Comment on the importance of the RFDS.

2. Discuss which effects on mankind great discoveries or inventions can have. Give examples from international or German history. — Discussing discoveries

3. It was John Flynn's belief that "If you start an idea, nothing can stop it." This resulted in the creation of the Flying Doctor Service. What about you? Do you have any good ideas concerning, for example, your life, family, friends, or your school, town or society as a whole? — Writing an essay
   a) Write an essay about your idea in which you describe what gave you this idea, what it is about, and how to put it into effect.
   b) If you do not have an idea, write an essay about a person who did have one and successfully realised it.

The Outback – Pearl and Peril of Australia

Uluru-Kata Tjuta National Park

Because of its extreme temperatures, the Outback is dangerous for people and animals, and is subject to bushfires. People living there feel relief when, in summer, temperatures drop down to the mid 30s. However, when it is really hot, 40–50 degrees and more, people suffer a lot. Every year there are incidents with people climbing Ayers Rock, although the Indigenous people ask them not to do so, as it is a holy place for them. Some tourists get heat strokes. Heat stroke shrinks your brain, and quite often these people become difficult to handle or do completely irrational things. Other people walk into the bush or to a salt lake equipped with just a bottle of water and wander, completely dehydrated, away from the path. Still others are bitten by spiders or snakes. Their legs swell up, their weight increases as a result of fluid retention, and they urgently need the help of a doctor – in serious cases, the help of the RFDS. Some people even die. As you can see below, the Outback is a wonderful place; however, you must be very careful.

Ayers Rock, or Uluru, the sacred rock of the Indigenous peoples

I never knew this about Australia

- The Outback covers about 80 per cent of Australia's total territory. It is famous for its remoteness and rugged landscapes. The Outback is the hottest area on the hottest continent of the world.
- In the Red Centre, temperatures typically range from 25 °C in winter up to 50–60 °C in summer, with night-time temperatures occasionally dropping to as low as 0 °C in winter. This makes the Outback extremely hard and dangerous for people and animals.
- A large part of the Outback lies in the Northern Territory (NT), which is characterised by two distinctive climate zones: a tropical zone in the north and deserts in the centre and south, including Alice Springs, Uluru and Kata Tjuta.
- In spite of this, Central Australia's fauna is surprisingly diverse. Kangaroos, wallabies, dingoes, emus, geckos, eagles, kites and many other unique animals live in desert habitats.
- Mining is the giant of NT industries, contributing 20 % of the Gross State Product. Tourism and agriculture (cattle, buffalo, field crops, fruit and vegetables) are also major contributors to NT economy.
- Alice Springs grew steadily after the arrival of the railway from Adelaide in 1929. Today, it is a busy town of about 27,000 people. Various films have been produced, and novels and television series written about it.

Indigenous man

Outback temperatures

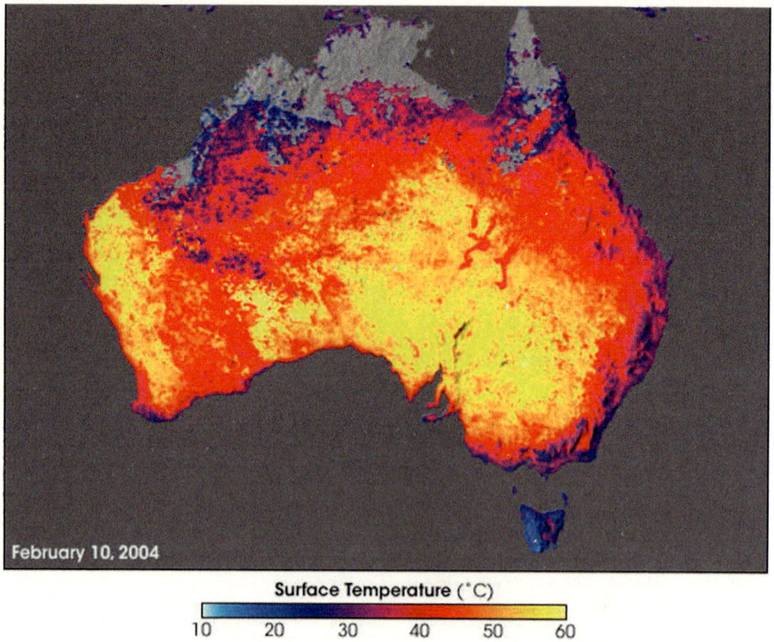

"Pukulpa pitjama Ananguku ngurakutu! Welcome to Aboriginal land! We, the traditional landowners of Uluru-Kata Tjuta National Park, are Yankunytjatjara and Pitjantjatjara people. We speak our language and teach it to our children. In our language, we call ourselves Anangu and we would like you to use that word too."
(from: Uluru-Kata Tjuta National Park. Visitor guide and maps. 2007)

Family reunion of Indigenous people

Activities

Comprehension

1. Name some of the characteristic features of the Outback.

2. What should tourists in the Outback pay special attention to?

Making a poster

3. Make sure you know these animals: kangaroo, wallaby, dingo, emu, gecko, eagle, kite. Design a poster containing facts about the Outback, including some of the animals living there.

Interpreting a physical map

4. Interpret the temperature map given above. What conclusions do you draw as to the quality of living in different regions of Australia?

The Rainbow Snake – Aboriginal Dreamtime Story

In Dreamtime, our ancestors walked the song lines of the Earth. The Earth they walked on was brown, flat and featureless[1]. The only colours shone in the sky after a storm. The distillation of colours hung there in the form of a rainbow. The rainbow dreamed and had longings in its heart. "I will go down and find a tribe who think as I do." The rainbow drank its own magic and writhed[2] into life as a snake. It was massively heavy and created valleys and hills as it travelled upon the Earth. The rain that fell was now channelled into rivers and lakes. One day the snake found a happy laughing tribe; it was mesmerised[3] by its music, and even though the tribe was initially[4] fearful, the snake coiled[5] itself around them and protected them. All was well until one night whilst[6] the snake was sleeping, two boys, mistaking the open mouth of the snake for a cave, crept inside for shelter from the rain. The snake felt something and swallowed! Realising what had happened, the snake tried to avoid being found out and slithered[7] away, hiding at the top of a mountain. The tribe's hunters went after it and, finding it sleeping, slit its side open. Out flew two beautiful birds with plumage[8] of many colours. The boys had been transformed. The snake was very angry and, in order to escape the rampage[9] of the venomous[10] Rainbow Snake, the people trans-

Children from years 5 and 6 of Jessie Younghusband School in Chichester, UK retold this traditional Aboriginal story and painted it in the style of Aboriginal Dot Art, assisted by famous British artist Jayne Sandys-Renton.

---

[1]**featureless** nothing particular to be seen [2]**to writhe** to twist one's body [3]**to be mesmerised** to find sb. or sth. very attractive [4]**initially** at the beginning [5]**to coil** to twist into a series of rings [6]**whilst** *fml.* while [7]**to slither** to slide twisting or moving from side to side [8]**plumage** feathers covering a bird's body [9]**rampage** rushing about in a wild and violent way [10]**venomous** poisonous, very angry

formed themselves into anything and everything. The snake exhausted itself and at last hurled[11] itself into the sea. It slithered into the setting sun. The following morning it was back in its place again as if it had never left, spanning the sky like a breath of peace; a miasma[12] of rain and sunlight.

[11]**to hurl** to throw sth. or oneself, to jump [12]**miasma** thick mist, dirty air

Activities

Retelling a story

1. Retell the Dreamtime story in your own words.

Investigating Dreamtime stories

2. Search the website www.dreamtime.net.au/dreaming/storylist.htm to read more Dreamtime stories and find out what role the Rainbow Snake and other characters play in Aboriginal mythology.

Analysing Creation stories

3. Using the information given on pages 54 and 55, analyse the Australian Aboriginal spiritual beliefs and compare these to other versions of Creation mythology.

Aboriginal sign language

Person

Man with spears

I never knew this about Australia

- About 40,000 to 80,000 years ago the first Aboriginal and Torres Strait Islander[1] peoples arrived in several waves via Indonesia. Tools found in Western Australia have been dated at 35,000 years – among the oldest so far discovered in Australia.
- It is estimated[2] there were some 750,000 people in Australia at the start of European settlement in 1788. This number declined[3] dramatically during the 19th and 20th centuries due to a number of factors, including diseases and conflict with the new settlers.
- On 30 June 2006, the Aboriginal and Torres Strait Islander population of the Commonwealth of Australia was estimated at 517,200, or 2.5 % of the total population. Two states, New South Wales (29 %) and Queensland (28 %), contained over half the Indigenous population. (Source: www.ausstats.abs.gov.au)

[1]**Torres Strait Islanders** Indigenous people living on the Torres Strait Islands that are part of Queensland [2]**to estimate** to give a number without calculating it exactly [3]**to decline** to fall, to go down

- Indigenous spiritual beliefs are founded on *tjukurrpa*, the Dreaming, also called Dreamtime. Dreaming spirits, who could change their form into animals, people or any physical feature[4], travelled across the country shaping the natural environment and establishing religious and moral systems for Indigenous Australians.
- Aboriginal people had and some still have a traditional sign language along with their spoken language.
- Indigenous Australians have long used fire as a land management tool. Since European settlement, fire has been both feared and harnessed[5] to clear land for agriculture and as a means of reducing risk to property from uncontrolled bushfires.
- Between 1910 and 1970, 10 – 30% of all Aboriginal children (up to 100,000 children) were forcibly taken from their families as part of a Federal and State Government policy to 'assimilate' Aboriginal children – especially those of mixed Aboriginal and European descent – into European society. They are known as the 'Stolen Generations'.
- Today, Indigenous cultures are diverse and form an essential[6] part of Australia's national identity. Indigenous people contribute significantly[7] to many fields including the arts, media and sport.
- The Australian Aboriginal flag was designed by Harold Thomas, an Indigenous elder[8], in 1971. The flag is flown at Aboriginal centres throughout Australia. The flag of the Torres Strait Islands was designed by Bernard Namok in 1992. The centre of the flag features a dancer's head-dress (*dharri*) and a five-pointed star which represents peace. The *dharri* is a national symbol of all Torres Strait Islanders. Nevertheless, it was not until 1995 that both flags were officially proclaimed as Flags of Australia.

People sitting

Rain

Emu

Snake

---

[4]**feature** *here* object [5]**to harness** to control and use a natural power [6]**essential** very important, necessary [7]**significantly** to a very high degree [8]**elder** the leader of an Aboriginal community who has gained recognition by the tribe because of a wealth of traditional knowledge and beliefs

Aboriginal flag: The yellow circle stands for the sun as the giver of life, black represents the people, red – the earth, thus symbolising Aboriginal unity.

Torres Strait Islander flag: Green represents the islands, blue the sea and black the people.

Willem Janszoon (ca. 1570 – 1630)

James Cook (1728 – 1779)

A Nation Is Born

The Dutch explorer Willem Janszoon and the Spanish sailor Luis Vaez de Torres were the first Europeans to discover Australia. In 1688, William Dampier became the first British explorer to land on the Australian northwest coast. It was not until 1770, however, that another Englishman, Captain James Cook, sailing with the Endeavour, claimed the east coast of Australia for the British Crown. Britain eventually decided to use the land as a penal colony[1]. The First Fleet of 11 ships, led by captain Arthur Phillip, which carried about 1,500 people arrived in Sydney Harbour on 26 January, 1788. It is on this day every year that Australia Day is celebrated. The convicts were soon joined by free immigrants, beginning in the early 1790s. The wool industry and the gold rushes of the 1850s, in particular, provided an impetus[2] for increasing numbers of free settlers to come to Australia.
Scarcity[3] of labour, the vastness[4] of the land and new wealth based on farming, mining and trade made Australia a land of opportunity. Yet during this period, Indigenous people suffered enormously. Death, illness, displacement and dispossession disrupted[5] their traditional lifestyles.
The Commonwealth of Australia was formed in 1901 through the federation of six states under a single constitution. The non-Indigenous population at the time of Federation was 3.8 million, while the estimated Indigenous population was around 93,000. The founders of the new nation believed they were creating something new and were anxious to avoid the pitfalls[6] of the old world. They wanted Australia to be harmonious, united and egalitarian, and had progressive ideas about human rights and the observance of democratic procedures.

---

[1] **penal colony** *Strafkolonie* [2] **impetus** an influence that makes sth. happen [3] **scarcity** a situation in which there is not enough of sth. [4] **vastness** extremely large or immense size [5] **to disrupt** to prevent sth. from continuing in its usual way [6] **pitfalls** difficulties, worries

Activities

Summing up facts

1. What are Willem Janszoon and James Cook famous for? Give a rough idea of how they contributed to Australian history.

Comparing timelines

2. Compare Australia's development in the 19th century with the history of Europe and the United States of America at the same time. Draw three historical timelines, and fill in the most important economic, political and social events on these continents.

Discussing national identity

3. Most people have come to Australia as immigrants. Just a few will proudly confess that their great-grandfathers were convicts. Given these different paths, who really is a 'True Blue Australian'? Is it the Indigenous people, or first, second, third generation immigrants? Or is it everybody who embraces the culture and lifestyle of Australia and chooses to be a citizen? Discuss and judge for yourself.

Writing an essay

4. Write an essay on the topic "Who is German?"

Stolen

Jane Harrison

This play shows what pain people who were separated from their Aboriginal parents long ago can feel still today. Standing to one side of Anne's bed, her parents are anxiously discussing something off stage.

This scene on the Great Australian Clock (Queen Victoria Building, Sydney) shows how Aboriginal children were forcibly removed from their parents.

FATHER: Princess, we need to tell you something ...
MOTHER: It's not been an easy decision for us ...
FATHER: We feel we've no choice and we want you to hear it from us.
MOTHER: We don't want you to hear rumours[1] ...
ANNE: What are you talking about?
MOTHER: We want you to know we'll always stand by you.
ANNE: What are you talking about ...?
FATHER: There's no easy way to tell you ... you know we adopted you, Anne. We chose you at the Cranby Children's Home.
ANNE: So ... I knew that ...
MOTHER: Anne, there's something else ... it's about your mother ... she's dying and she wants to see you and ... she's an *Aboriginal* lady.
ANNE: Why haven't you told me that she's –?
MOTHER: (*tentatively*[2]) – Aboriginal?
ANNE: Alive! And that she wants to see me?
MOTHER: Oh. (MOTHER *starts to weep*.)
FATHER: We thought it was for the best. You know we love you like our own daughter.
MOTHER: We love you and want the best for you.
FATHER: Anne, there's no reason why anything should change. You only have to see her ... once.
MOTHER: No one need ever know.
ANNE: I know. And I want to know why you didn't tell me about this before.
MOTHER: (*sobbing*[3]) The shame ...
ANNE: (*angrily*) You should be ashamed – (Anne's FATHER *draws himself upright and puts his arm around* MOTHER.)
FATHER: We've nothing to be ashamed of. We've always acted in your best interest! Look what you've done to your mother! (*They walk away, talking amongst themselves. Alone,* ANNE *is so confused.*)
ANNE: Mum ... Dad! Mum! Dad! Why? This is a nightmare!

[1] **rumour** *Gerücht* [2] **tentatively** in an uncertain way [3] **to sob** to cry noisily

Activities

1. Bearing in mind what was said about the 'Stolen Generations' on page 55, analyse the situation in the play. What feelings do the protagonist and her parents reveal? How did the problem come about? What solution to the problem do you see? Discuss. — *Analysing a situation*

2. Imagine you are Anne. Write her diary entry for this day. — *Writing a diary entry*

The Burnum Burnum Declaration

Burnum Burnum

Burnum Burnum (fifth from left), together with Prime Minister Harold Holt (third from left) in 1967

Burnum Burnum (1936–1997) "was an activist, rugby player, actor, author, dreamer and respected Aboriginal elder. Removed from his parents at the age of three months and named Harry Penrith, he spent his early years in children's homes, where he was raised to believe he was white. [...] On Australia Day 1988, he famously declared Aboriginal possession of England, raising the Aboriginal flag on the English coast at Dover."[1]

I, Burnum Burnum, being a nobleman of ancient Australia do hereby take possession of England on behalf of the Aboriginal People.
In claiming this colonial outpost, we wish no harm to you natives, but assure you that we are here to bring you good manners, refinement and an opportunity to make a Koompartoo – 'a fresh start'. Henceforth, an Aboriginal face shall appear on your coins and stamps to signify our sovereignty over this domain. For the more advanced, we bring the complex language of the Pitjantjajara; we will teach you how to have a spiritual relationship with the Earth and show you how to get bush tucker[2]! We do not intend to souvenir, pickle and preserve the heads of 2000 of your people, nor to publicly display the skeletal remains of your Royal Highness, as was done to our Queen Truganinni for 80 years. Neither do we intend to poison your water holes, lace your flour with strychnine or introduce you to highly toxic drugs. Based on our 50,000 year heritage, we acknowledge the need to preserve the Caucasian race as of interest to antiquity, although we may be inclined to conduct experiments by measuring the size of your skulls for levels of intelligence. We pledge not to sterilise your women, nor to separate your children from their families. We give an absolute undertaking that you shall not be placed onto the mentality of government handouts for the next five generations but you will enjoy the full benefits of Aboriginal equality. At the end of two hundred years, we will make a Treaty to validate occupation by peaceful means and not by conquest. Finally, we solemnly promise not to make a quarry of England and export your valuable minerals back to the old country Australia, and we vow[3] never to destroy three-quarters of your trees, but to encourage Earth Repair Action to unite people, communities, religions and nations in a common productive peaceful purpose.

[1]from: Anita Heiss, Peter Minter (eds.): Macquarie PEN Anthology of Aboriginal Literature, Allen & Unwin, Sydney 2008, pp. 124–125 [2]**tucker** Aboriginal word for food [3]**to vow** to make a serious promise

Activities

Discussing the message of a text

1. What does Burnum Burnum declare? What is the author's intention? Comment on the text.

Analysing style

2. Analyse the stylistic devices the author uses. Give examples.

The Great Ocean Road – A Symbol of National Identity

'he Diggers' – sculpture in honour of the
uilders of the Great Ocean Road

'Penguin Parade' on Phillip Island near Melbourne

Part of the most famous sight along the Great Ocean Road: The Twelve Apostles

ackpackers on tour

Eucalyptus wood – Australia boasts more than 800 species of gum trees

Emu with her chicks

oala in Cape Otway National Park

Golden wattle – the national flower of Oz and basis for its sporting colours (green and gold)

Activities

1. Describe the pictures. What natural beauties do they show?
2. Search the web to find out who built the Great Ocean Road, why it became a symbol of national identity, and why it attracts thousands of tourists every year. Prepare a presentation.

NB: 'Digger' is a slang word for 'gold miner' or 'Australian Soldier'.

The Nation Apologises

In February 2007, the newly-elected Prime Minister of the Commonwealth of Australia, Kevin Rudd, made it the first item of his new government agenda to give an official apology to the Stolen Generations. The apology received widespread support from people in Australia and abroad. Read the beginning of his speech. What does it say about the mistreatment of Aboriginals in the past, and what future does it promise?

People listening to the Sorry Speech

I move[1]:

That today we honour the Indigenous peoples of this land, the oldest continuing cultures in human history. We reflect on their past mistreatment. We reflect in particular on the mistreatment of those who were stolen generations – this blemished[2] chapter in our nation's history. The time has now come for the nation to turn a new page in Australia's history by righting the wrongs of the past and so moving forward with confidence to the future.

We apologise for the laws and policies of successive parliaments and governments that have inflicted[3] profound grief[4], suffering and loss on these our fellow Australians.

We apologise especially for the removal of Aboriginal and Torres Strait Islander children from their families, their communities and their country. For the pain, suffering and hurt of these stolen generations, their descendants and for their families left behind, we say sorry. To the mothers and the fathers, the brothers and the sisters, for the breaking up of families and communities, we say sorry. And for the indignity[5] and degradation thus inflicted on a proud people and a proud culture, we say sorry.

We the parliament of Australia respectfully request that this apology be received in the spirit in which it is offered as part of the healing of the nation. For the future we take heart, resolving that this new page in the history of our great continent can now be written. We today take this first step by acknowledging the past and laying claim to a future that embraces all Australians. A future where this parliament resolves that the injustices of the past must never, never happen again.

---

[1]**to move** *fml. here* to officially make a proposal, esp. in parliament [2]**blemished** imperfect, ruined [3]**to inflict** to make someone suffer [4]**grief** extreme sadness [5]**indignity** *Demütigung*

Activities

Listing apologies

1. What does the Australian government have to say sorry for? Make a list.

Taking notes and giving a summary

2. Watch the video clip for more information on the speech: www.smh.com.au/multimedia/2008/national/australia-says-sorry/main.html. Take notes on the speech, and give an oral summary.

I Am Proud

Oodgeroo Noonuccal

"The author of this poem, Oodgeroo Noonuccal, was born Kathleen Jean Mary Ruska on 3 November, 1920, on North Stradbroke Island, country of the Noonuccal tribe. She attended Dulwich Primary, left school and became a domestic[1] in Brisbane at the age of 13. [...] Oodgeroo's work has been recognised with numerous awards[2]. She also held an honorary doctorate of letters (Macquarie University) and was awarded the degree of Doctor of the University from Griffith University." (from: www.womenaustralia.info)

I am black of skin among whites,
And I am proud,
Proud of race and proud of skin.
I am broken and poor,
Dressed in rags from white man's back,
But do not think I am ashamed.
Spears could not contend against guns and we were mastered,
But there are things they could not plunder and destroy.
We were conquered but never subservient[3],
We were compelled[4] but never servile.
Do not think I cringe[5] as white men cringe to whites.
I am proud,
Thought humble[6] and poor and without a home ...
So was Christ.

Oodgeroo Noonuccal, 1974

[1]**domestic** *old* a servant who performs household tasks, esp. in a large house [2]**award** a prize or money given to sb. for their good work [3]**subservient** always doing what other people want you to do [4]**to compel** to force sb. to do sth. [5]**to cringe** *here* to feel embarrassed [6]**humble** modest and respectful

Activities

1. Read the poem, and then consider who the speaker in the poem is, and how the person describes life. — Comprehension

2. Read the poem again. This time, pay special attention to the adjectives and verbs the author uses. Which feelings do they reflect? — Feeling words

3. Recite the poem. Try to read it out with expression and emotion.

4. Compare Oodgeroo Noonuccal's poem to Burnum Burnum's 'Declaration' (p. 58). Both are Aboriginal-born people. What feelings do they reveal, and what are their messages? Discuss. — Comparing two statements

Australia's Government

Kevin Rudd (Labor Party) was sworn in as the 26th Prime Minister of Australia on 3 December 2007.

Her Excellency Ms Quentin Bryce AC, Governor-General since 2008

The Commonwealth of Australia was founded in 1901. Its Constitution establishes a federal system involving a national government and state governments. The country is a parliamentary democracy as Australians elect a national parliament. It is also a constitutional monarchy as the Queen (or King) of Great Britain is the official Head of State. However, the monarch does not play a day-to-day role in Australian government. Instead, the Governor-General, appointed by the Queen (or King) on the advice of the Prime Minister, is her or his representative in Australia.

The Constitution establishes three separate arms of national government – a legislative arm, an executive arm and a judicial arm – and distributes powers between them. The Government of Australia has its seat in Canberra, Australia's capital.

The Commonwealth Parliament is the law-making body. It has two 'Houses' – the House of Representatives, which has 150 members, and the Senate (with 76 senators), in which elected members consider proposed laws and conduct[1] all the business of the Parliament. Read how the Commonwealth Government is formed.

All Australian citizens aged 18 and over are required to enrol[2] to vote and voting is compulsory

A general election is held

The Government is formed
The leader of the party that wins the majority of seats in the House of Representatives becomes the Head of the Government, or Prime Minister. The political party that wins the second largest number of seats is known as the Opposition.

Ministers are appointed
The Prime Minister chooses members or senators to become ministers. Ministers are chosen for all portfolios[3], states and territories.

The Cabinet is formed
Ministers with the most senior portfolios make up the Cabinet, which is the decision-making body of the Government.

[1]**to conduct** *here* to carry out, to do [2]**to enrol** *here* to officially arrange to take part in elections [3]**portfolio** responsibility of a minister

Activities

Comprehension

1. Explain why Australia is a parliamentary and constitutional monarchy.
2. What are the different functions of Parliament, the Prime Minister and the Head of State in Australia? Explain.

Using a mindmap or flowchart to give a talk

3. To understand the structure of Australia's government better, draw a mindmap or flowchart. Then give a talk on how this government works.

Politics and Economy in the 20th Century

Australia has a strong economy with a per capita GDP[1] on par[2] with highly developed European countries. Coal, iron ore, gold, meat, wool, wheat, transport equipment are the main export products. This economic strength is mainly the result of a successful development during the 20th century. Read the following two texts on Australia's political and economic development.

About 1900, Australia became known as the social laboratory of the world. Political rights were widespread. Most men had had the vote from the 1850s; women then gained the vote, in South Australia first in 1894, and in the new Commonwealth in 1902. Governments were active in protecting wages and living conditions, giving help to farmers and pensions to the old. As the Labor Party grew, all other parties combined into a Liberal Party in 1910.

One difference between the parties was that Labor was more ready to use the government to help the workers and small farmers while its more radical members wanted government to take over industries so they were not run for profit. The Liberals were suspicious[3] of government and encouraged individual enterprise while the more radical wanted to roll back the level of government activity. Despite these party differences, the amount of government activity in the economy in the first 70 years of the 20th century was very high. If wages[4] were to be kept high, manufacturers had to be protected from foreign competition so that they could pay them. Farmers who sold their produce[5] in world markets could only pay high wages and afford the high cost of manufactured goods if the government assisted in the marketing of their crops[6].

The Country Party, formed after World War I, at first wanted to reduce protection for local industry. Failing that, it argued that farmers, as the earners of export income, should get every possible assistance. In the 1980s, the Country Party changed its name to the National Party. Usually, it acts in coalition with the Liberal Party. From the 1980s, more and more experts argued that the economy would grow more strongly if it was not protected in so many ways by the government. During the 1980s and 1990s, Australian governments took this advice. They opened up the economy by floating[7] the dollar, cutting back on tariff protection, selling off government enterprises and abandoning[8] the central control of wages. Both major parties now see Australia's future in a global economy with prosperity[9] depending on leaving industries to the discipline of the market.

Australian parties:

Australian Labor Party

Liberal Party

The Nationals

Minor parties:
Australian Democrats
Australian Greens
One Nation
Family First Party

[1]**GDP** Gross Domestic Product, *Bruttoinlandsprodukt* [2]**on par** at the same level [3]**suspicious** distrustful [4]**wages** money paid for work [5]**produce** food or other things that have been produced on a farm to be sold [6]**crop** the amount of food produced from the land in a season [7]**floating** allowing the value of a country's money to change freely in relation to the value of money from other countries [8]**to abandon** to stop doing sth. [9]**prosperity** economic success and social well-being

Oz has produced more than ten Nobel Prize winners in various fields.

German backpacker at a plantation in Lakeland

Sydney Port

Quarry[1] near Melbourne

Fishing port, Brisbane

Australia – Neither Down nor Under

The following text, which was written by an independent international organisation in 2008, proves that today, Australia is indeed a highly-developed country on par with the leading European states.

Australia is currently the world's 14th largest economy by nominal GDP, with a size of $ 889 billion in 2007. Following a recession in the 1980s, Australia had enjoyed 16 years of uninterrupted growth, aided by growing demand for commodities[2] and robust government policies. GDP long term growth has averaged 4.4 %, with a 3.3 % average between 2003 and 2007, but is expected to drop to the 2 – 3 % range over the next five years.
Australia is a western-style market economy. It is a major exporter of natural gas, coal, iron, bauxite, copper, tin, gold, silver, uranium, tungsten[3], mineral sands, lead, zinc, opals, diamonds, grain, wool, meat and food products. Although the agricultural and mining sectors are small, 4.7 % of GDP combined, they contribute approximately 65 % of exports. In 2007, Australia imported $ 228 billion of goods and services and exported $ 216 billion.
The main export partners are Japan, China, South Korea, the US and India, and the main import partners are the US, China, Japan, Singapore, and Germany. Inflation is currently rising as it is in most countries of the world. It stood at 4.2 % at the end of last year and is likely to continue to be above the 2 – 3 % target set by the Bank of Australia.
The country has a favorable trade balance, but has a current account deficit of 5.8 % that is expected to continue until 2012 according to the International Monetary Fund. This reflects large interest[4] payments against foreign debt. While traditionally tied to Europe and the US, Australia is now dependent on Asia for its economic well-being. In particular, it partners with Japan for capital financing, particularly in the mining industry, and with China as its primary export partner. The economy has also been supported by a housing market boom and a strong national currency.

[1] **quarry** a place where stone or sand are dug out of the ground [2] **commodity** Ware, Rohstoff [3] **tungsten** *Wolfram* [4] **interest** *Zins*

Activities

Comprehension

1. How did Australia develop politically and economically in the 19th and 20th centuries, and what are its economic strengths today? Describe in your own words.

Comparing statistical data

2. Using the data given in the text above and searching the web, create a statistical chart in which you compare Australia to other countries.

Giving a presentation

3. Read the texts on pp. 63 and 64 and search the web for more information on Australia's politics and economy. Give a presentation.

NEW ZEALAND

Getting started

Auckland

Coromandel Rain Forest

Buller Gorge Swingbridge

Māori

Fox Glacier

New Zealand's 'white gold'

- Describe the pictures. Which beautiful regions and landscapes does New Zealand boast?
- Which picture arouses your particular interest? Why?

New Zealand – My First Encounter

I never knew this about New Zealand

New Zealand

- ... is an island country in the south-west Pacific. It is located around 1,600 kilometres away from the eastern coast of Australia, its nearest neighbour. Comparable in size (270,500 sq km) to Great Britain, its main territory is about 2,000 km long and 550 km across at its widest point.
- ... has been inhabited by *Māori*[1] since about AD 1000. The country was first mapped by Abel Tasman in 1642–1643, and later by James Cook (1769–1778). The term 'Nova Zeelandia' was coined by Dutch cartographers after Zeeland, a province in the Netherlands.
- ... was settled by the British and became a colony of the Crown in 1840. The Treaty of Waitangi guaranteed the Māori full possession of their land in exchange for their recognition of British sovereignty.
- ... became an independent nation in 1948. However, the country is a member of the British Commonwealth, as is Australia. The indigenous Māori name of the country is *Aotearoa*[2], which means 'long white cloud'.
- ... has a multicultural population of 4.3 million people (September 2009), the majority of which are of British descent. The country's indigenous Māori, a Polynesian people, make up around 15 % of the population.
- ... comprises two main islands, the North Island and South Island, and numerous smaller islands. It is a land of great contrasts and diversity. They include active volcanoes, spectacular caves, deep glacier lakes, beautiful valleys, exciting fiords, long sandy beaches, and the spectacular snow-capped peaks of the Southern Alps.
- ... is home to the long-beaked, flightless kiwi, the country's national bird. For this reason, a widespread nickname for New Zealanders is 'Kiwi' (spoken with an English 'w'). The NZ Dollar, too, is often called 'kiwi', as is the juicy kiwifruit which, although originally grown in China, was first given this name in New Zealand because of its kiwi-like hairy, brown skin.

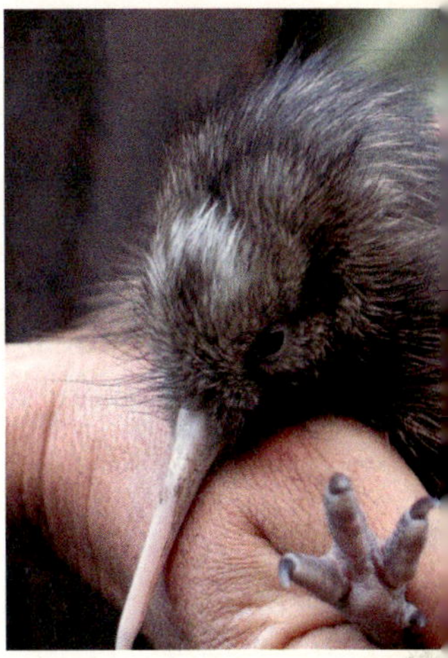

[1] **Māori** [ˈmaʊrɪ] the name means 'normal, ordinary'; ā is a long vowel [2] **Aotearoa** [aoteaˈroa] the word consists of three parts: *ao* = cloud, *tea* = white, *roa* = long

Activities

Comprehension

1. Which meanings does the word 'kiwi' have?
2. What do you know about New Zealand's population and languages?

Making a fact sheet

3. Make a fact sheet of what you already know about Aotearoa. Keep this record until you have finished the New Zealand course. Later, you can compare your knowledge about the 'long white cloud' before and after you have completed this course.

Searching the web

4. Search the web for discoverers and founders of New Zealand. Find out what they are famous for and give a talk about each of them: Abel Tasman, James Cook, Edward Gibbon Wakefield, William Hobson.

The Legend of Māui

A Māori ancestral figure

Māori mythology says that the North and South Islands of New Zealand came from the time of Māui, who was a demigod[1]. Legend has it that he and his brothers were fishing from their canoe (which formed the South Island) when he caught a giant fish and pulled it in from the sea. While he was not looking, his brothers stole the fish and chopped[2] it up. This great fish became the North Island, and thus, the Māori name for the North Island is *Te Ika O Māui* (The Fish of Māui). A look at a map of the North Island shows that it really does resemble[3] an exotic fish. The Māori believe the far north to be the tail of the fish and Wellington Harbour the mouth.

Haere Mai! – Te Reo Māori

"Haere mai!" This is Māori and means "Welcome!" The Māori language (*te reo Māori*) was the predominant language of New Zealand until the 1840s. At that time, English settlers brought their language, English, to the islands. In the late 19th century, English became the only official language in New Zealand. The use of Māori in school and practising Māori traditions were even forbidden. Most Māori learnt English, although up until World War II, many of them still spoke Māori at home. By the 1980s, less than 20 % of the Indigenous population knew the language well enough to be considered[4] native speakers, and for many of those people, Māori was even no longer the language of the home. Only then did Māori leaders begin to recognise the dangers of the loss of their traditions and to initiate language and culture recovery[5] programmes.

[1] **demigod** half god, half human [2] **to chop** to cut into smaller pieces [3] **to resemble** to look like sb. or sth. [4] **to consider** to think of sb. or sth. in a particular way or to have a particular opinion [5] **recovery** the process of returning to a normal condition after a period of trouble or difficulty

Today Māori has roughly 160,000 speakers (more than one fourth of the indigenous population, which numbers almost 570,000). The Māori language enjoys official language status in New Zealand. That means, for example, that New Zealand citizens can request[6] to be addressed in their mother tongue in a court of law, and the court is expected to provide a translator. The Māori Television Service began broadcasting on 28 March, 2004. Most public services, however, are available only in English. In spite of this, there are many Māori words used in New Zealand English, such as *Pākeha* meaning non-Māori, or people of European descent, or *Te Pāpa* (meaning 'the homeland'), the name of the National Museum of New Zealand in Wellington.

[6]**to request** to ask for sth. in a formal way

Students from New Plymouth Girls' High School performing a traditional Māori dance

Activities

1. Look at the map of New Zealand and try to make out the tail and the mouth of the fish. Try retelling the Māori legend in your own words.
   Comprehension

2. Compare the history of the Māori language to the fate of minority languages such as Welsh in the UK, or Friesian or Sorbian in Germany.
   Investigating minority languages

This is "Hello!" in Māori: "Kia ora!"

Treaty of Waitangi

The Treaty of Waitangi, signed on 6 February, 1840 by William Hobson[1] and marked by Māori chiefs, is a milestone in New Zealand history. Read the text of the Treaty and a story about Māori resistance to it. Then do the tasks given on the next page.

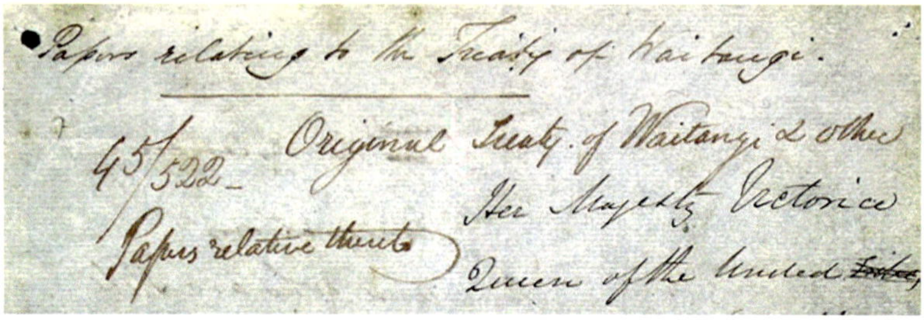
Papers relating to the Treaty of Waitangi.
45/522 Original Treaty of Waitangi & other Papers relative thereto
Her Majesty Victoria Queen of the United

This copy shows a part of W. Hobson's papers relating to the Treaty of Waitangi.

Victoria, the Queen of England, in her concern to protect the chiefs and the subtribes of New Zealand and in her desire to preserve their chieftainship and their lands to them and to maintain peace and good order considers it just[2] to appoint an administrator who will negotiate with the people of New Zealand to the end that their chiefs will agree to the Queen's Government being established over all parts of this land and (adjoining) islands and also because there are many of her subjects[3] already living on this land and others yet to come. So the Queen desires to establish a government so that no evil will come to Māori and European living in a state of lawlessness. So the Queen has appointed me, William Hobson, a Captain in the Royal Navy, to be Governor for all parts of New Zealand [...] and presents to the chiefs of the Confederation, chiefs of the subtribes of New Zealand and other chiefs [who] these laws set out here:

KO TE TUATAHI
The Chiefs of the Confederation and all the Chiefs who have not joined that Confederation give absolutely to the Queen of England for ever the complete government over their land.

KO TE TUARUA
The Queen of England agrees to protect the chiefs, the subtribes and all the people of New Zealand in the unqualified exercise[4] of their chieftainship over their lands, villages and all their treasures. But on the other hand the Chiefs of the Confederation and all the Chiefs will sell land to the Queen at a price agreed to by the person owning it and by the person buying it (the latter being) appointed by the Queen as her purchase.

KO TE TUATORU
For this agreed arrangement therefore concerning the Government of the Queen, the Queen of England will protect all the ordinary people of New Zealand and will give them the same rights and duties of citizenship as the people of England. *(signed) William Hobson Consul & Lieut. Governor*

---

[1]**William Hobson** was appointed Lieutenant-Governor of the colony and had the task of taking possession of New Zealand with the consent of the Māori chiefs [2]**just** *adj.* morally right and fair [3]**subjects** *here* people [4]**unqualified exercise** *uneingeschränkte Ausübung*

The face tattoo worn by the Māori is called moko.

Parihaka – A Symbol of Protest

Not all tribes signed the Treaty and many showed active or passive resistance. Read about the most powerful of these movements.

Through the remainder[1] of the 1870s, with the exception of the people of Parihaka[2], the lot of the Māori continued to decline[3]. Finally defeated – if not conclusively – on the battlefields, they were pressured to adopt European habits, but this caused confusion as they tried to live within two cultures, and their general health deteriorated. Parihaka was the shining exception. Under the strong leadership of Christian pacifists and prophets, Te Whiti o Rongomai and Tohu Kakahi, both of Te Atiawa and Taranaki, the community took what it wanted from European culture, but then insisted on a philosophy of *turangawaewae* – a physical, cultural and spiritual separation. They ignored the fact that their land was officially confiscated. The people of Parihaka wanted to be left alone. None of the Taranaki tribes had signed the Treaty of Waitangi, and Te Whiti, insisting the confiscations were illegal, was determined to assert[4] ownership in a peaceful way. By 1878, the increasing European demand for land, and pressure of debts, prompted[5] the Government to send the surveyors[6] on to the Waimate Plains to mark out land for settlement and a road around the coast. By February 1879, the surveyors' job was almost complete, but promised Māori reserves had not materialised. As a final insult[7], they ran a line through the settlement of legendary warrior Titokowaru, trampling crops in the process. Titokowaru's people responded by ripping up miles of survey pegs[8]. Three days later, the first 16,000 acres of the Waimate Plains was advertised for sale, but Tohu's men promptly escorted the surveyors off the land and the sale was postponed[9].

Te Whiti and Tohu, leaders of what had become the most populous and prosperous Māori community in New Zealand, would no longer accept attacks on their autonomy, so they embarked[10] on the next stage of their campaign of passive resistance against the surveyors.

Traditional Māori wood carvings in Rotorua (above) and in the Dunedin Otage Museum (below)

---

[1]**remainder** the rest, *here* the last years [2]**Parihaka** a small Māori community in the Taranaki region [3]**to decline** to become gradually worse, to deteriorate [4]**to assert** *here* to defend [5]**to prompt** to force [6]**surveyor** *Landvermesser* [7]**insult** offence [8]**peg** stick [9]**to postpone** to change a planned action to a later date [10]**to embark** *here* to start

Activities

1. Who were Te Whiti o Rongomai and Tohu Kakahi and what did they fight against and what for? — Comprehension

2. Was the Māori's fight successful in the end? Try to give a first answer to this question. However, keep this question in mind. You will be able to answer it more definitely when you have finished this book. — Analysing and judging a historical movement

3. Give a speech on the Treaty of Waitangi and the Parihaka movement. Explain why they are of particular importance to New Zealand. — Giving a speech

Māori Then and Today

Māori show in Tamaki Māori village, Rotorua

I never knew this about New Zealand

- Together with the *Pākeha*[1] Māori represent a considerable part of New Zealand's society. Not only is their colourful folklore very popular with Kiwis and tourists alike, but the Māori today play an important role in every field.
- Since 1975, the Māori have had the right to choose their members in the Parliament. There are many outstanding talented Māori politicians who have helped people through the difficulties associated with changing from the old Māori way of life to the new ways of the modern world.
- The last few decades of the 20th century saw a significant resurgence of interest in, and use of, the Māori language. Much of this revival can be attributed to the establishment of *kohanga reo* (language nests) for Māori preschoolers. The first *kohanga reo* was set up in 1981; six years later, 522 language nests, with more than 10,000 children enrolled, had been established throughout the country.
- In the latest census, the proportion of Māori stating they were unemployed fell from 16.8 percent in 2001 to 11.0 percent in 2006. At that time, the Marlborough Region had the lowest unemployment rate for Māori (4.7%).
- Māori athletes typically perform excellently in rugby, basketball, tennis, golf and other sports.
- The old Māori way of life has almost disappeared. The life of the Māori today is not really different from that of the *Pākeha*. They live in the same kinds of houses and do the same kind of work. However, most Māori communities have a club that promotes their traditional culture, song and dance. They take part in Māori action songs and *haka*[2] teams and go to many meetings at the *marae*[3]. Many speak Māori and English. Above all, they feel that they are Māori and not *Pākeha*.

Did you know?

The longest place name in New Zealand is

Taumatawhakatangihangakoauauotamateaturipukaka-pikimaungahoronukupokaiwhenuakitanatahu

(85 letters). This place lies in the Province of Hawke's Bay on the North Island. The word is Māori and means: "The hill where the great traveller (Chief) Tamatea with the bony knees, who slid and climbed mountains, played his flute to his beloved."

Watch New Zealand sportsmen perform a *haka* on TV or on the Internet.

---

[1]**Pākeha** [pāke'ha] New Zealander of non-Māori descent, usually European [2]**haka** ritual dance performed for different reasons such as encouragement, amusement, frigthening an enemy, etc. [3]**marae** [ma'raɪ] sacred place or building of the Māori

Māori Ethnic Population – Te Momo Iwi[1] Māori

According to data of New Zealand's official statistics agency, at the time of the 2006 Census, there were 14.6 percent of the total population who identified with the Māori ethnic group and lived in New Zealand. The Māori ethnic population includes those people who stated Māori as being their sole[2] ethnic group or one of several ethnic groups they belong to. Just over half (52.8 percent) of all people in the Māori ethnic group identified Māori as their only ethnicity, 42.2 percent of Māori stated that they identified with European ethnic groups, only a small percentage gave New Zealander, Pacific, Asian or several nations as their ethnic groups. The Māori ethnic population in New Zealand grew from 434,847 in 1991 to 565,329 in 2006.

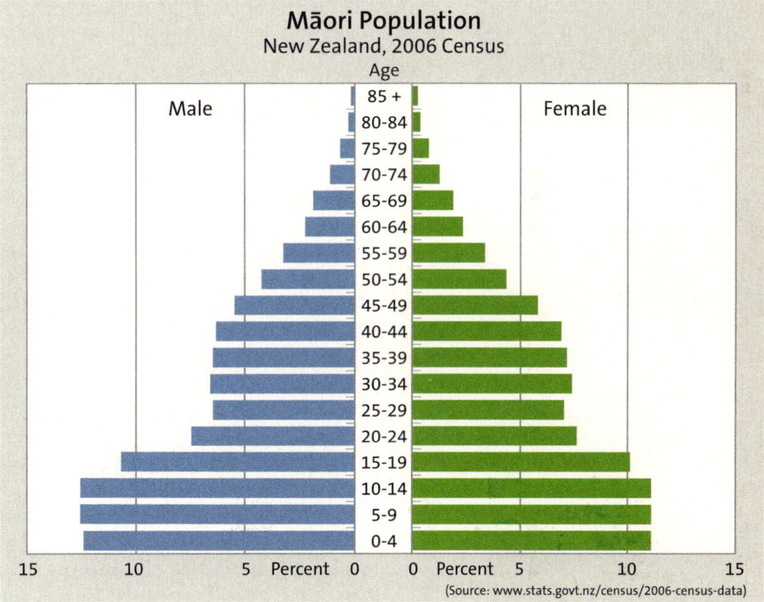

[1]**te** the **momo** breed, kind **iwi** (spoken with an English 'w') tribe [2]**sole** only

Activities

1. Read the text on page 68/69 about the development of the Māori identity and analyse the bar chart on this page. Organise the numbers from the text in the form of two pie charts, then prepare a talk in which you interpret the numbers given in your charts. In your talk, answer this question: How has the Māori identity developed in recent years?

Organising statistical data

2. Compare the bar chart of the Māori population with the age distribution of the population of Germany. Which differences do you notice? What might be the reasons for these differences? Discuss.

Comparing statistics

3. Listen to New Zealand's national anthem and analyse its message: http://folksong.ore.nz/e_ihowa_atua.

Listening to the national anthem

Māori Culture in New Zealand and Abroad

"Kia ora!" Now read the following extracts from articles published in NZ newspapers and magazines that show you how well integrated into everyday life Māori and their culture are in Aotearoa and abroad.

Māori of the Te Arawa tribe (Rotorua Visitor Guide)

Feel the spirit – Manaakitanga

It's our Rotorua catcher[1], and it holds a pretty powerful promise. On the one hand, the expression is your invitation to experience the essence – the spirit of this extraordinary slice of New Zealand. 'Feel the Spirit', or in Māori *'Manaakitanga'* is a challenge, a responsibility upon us as your hosts. *Manaakitanga* is a deep-rooted concept in Māori culture. It implies guardianship over our land (*whenua*), treasures (*taaonga*), people (*tangata*) and you, our visitors (*manuhiri*). When visitors first arrive, *Manaakitanga* begins. From that point on, it is our job to ensure that we give the very best of ourselves, or our history, of our time. *Manaakitanga* is a tradition of which we are fiercely proud and a role we take seriously. It is a very special feeling.

THE UNIVERSITY OF AUCKLAND
NEW ZEALAND

Leaders get experience

More than 100 Māori and Pasifika[2] students in the Faculty of Arts have been recognised through the *tuakana*[3] art leadership programme at Auckland University. Launched[4] last year, it recognises Māori and Pasifika undergraduates who excel[5] in their academic[6] pursuits. They are invited to participate in the year-long programme, which offers ongoing academic support and preparation for postgraduate studies. The programme also provides opportunities for internships[7] with various organisations across the Auckland region.

Children of Kohanga Reo o Ranana performing a *haka* while being filmed by the BBC

tamariki[8] on TV

The young members of Kohanga Reo o Ranana, a group dedicated to keeping the Kiwi identity alive in London, recently had an opportunity to showcase the Māori culture after they were filmed by the BBC children's television network [...]. Kohanga Reo o Ranana, a group that runs workshops for children and meets at New Zealand House on Saturday mornings, comes under the auspices of the Ngati Ranana Māori Culture Club and was established by a dedicated group of New Zealand parents who wanted their children to know about their heritage even though they were growing up so far away from 'home'.

---

[1] **catcher** *here* eye-catcher [2] **Pasifika** (*Māori*) people of Pacific nation heritage living in New Zealand [3] **tuakana** (*Māori*) peer teaching [4] **to launch** to start [5] **to excel** to be very good at doing sth. or better than others [6] **academic pursuits** *here* university studies [7] **internship** a short-term job students do to gain experience [8] **tamariki** (*Māori*) children up to 14 years

Kiwis one short in medal hunt – Paralympics

The final day of competition for New Zealand athletes at the Beijing Paralympics ended painfully short of the team's 13-medal target. It was left up to powerlifter[1] George Taamaru of Auckland to bring the medal count beyond five gold medals, three silvers and four bronzes on the last day for the Kiwis last week. Taamaru, 35, lifting the 100 kg-plus category, had every chance to win a medal but was cut short[2] by some curious judging that saw him given two 'no-lifts'. He decided to go for broke[3] on his final lift with a total of 235 kg, which would have given him silver, but it proved too much. Team Chef de Mission Duane Kale said, while it was disappointing not to reach the 13 medal target, the team performed well and things looked positive for the London Paralympics in 2012.

Strong man "big George" Taamaru

Māori heritage in Great Britain

James Schuster, a Māori heritage advisor to New Zealand's Historic Places Trust, will fly to England this month to advise Cambridge University staff on how to move and restore a flagpole that was carved[4] by his great-great grandfather, Tene Waitere, and has been standing in obscurity[5] at a Portsmouth naval shore base for 85 years. The flagpole, or *pouhaki*, which features intricate[6] patterns of figures holding traditional weapons, was presented to Edward, Prince of Wales, in Rotorua during an official visit to New Zealand in 1920. In recent years, Waitere has been recognized as one of the greatest Māori carvers of the colonial period (some of his works are now located in London's British Museum and museums in Hamburg, Stuttgart and St. Petersburg) and the flagpole is thought to be one of his oldest carvings – and the only one located outside of New Zealand.

8 m high flagpole in the Cambridge Museum of Archaeology and Anthropology

[1]**powerlifter** athlete who does a weightlifting sport consisting of three events [2]**to cut short** to stop sb. from doing what they wanted to [3]**to go for broke** to take big risks [4]**to carve** to cut figures or patterns in wood or stone [5]**in obscurity** forgotten [6]**intricate** containing many small parts that form one complex work

Activities

Comprehension

1. How does the first text explain the term *Manaakitanga*?
2. Sum up in one-sentence statements what each of the five articles deals with. Begin your summaries like this: "The text '(title)' is about ..."

Analyzing NZ English

3. What is the frequent use of Māori words in everyday life a sign of?
4. Surf the web for more information about these Māori terms that are frequently used in New Zealand English: marae, haka, hongi, moko, pouhaki. Make a poster which explains and illustrates them.

Virtually visiting 'Te Papa'

5. If you want to know more about Māori life and culture, visit NZ's National Museum 'Te Papa': www.tepapa.govt.nz. Write a letter in which you give reasons why it is worth visiting.

Schools in New Zealand

A High School Year in Aotearoa

"Tuition[1] and boarding fees are high, of course, but spending a high school year in New Zealand is an unforgettable experience!"
(Maria, a German student)
Read the e-mail Maria sent to a friend of hers.

Hi Mel,

Happy New Year! I was away on holiday in Queenstown around New Years Day --- but now I'm back in New Plymouth, I can finally answer your e-mail and send you some brief news. Term 1 begins soon, but today is the 6th of January, 2009! It's my 18th birthday!!! ☺☺☺ I am planning to have a cool party this evening!

My teachers here are quite alright. In year 12, we only have to take five subjects. I've chosen English and Maths (both are compulsory), Latin, French and Visual Arts. There are a lot more subjects to choose from than we have at our school in Germany.

Every morning we have 'form time'. Our form teacher and my form class get together and talk about what has been happening around the school or what needs to be done. About twice a week, the whole school gets together during form time for 'admin'. That is short for 'administration' and means that the principal talks to the whole school about our sports teams and projects that are taking place inside and outside of the school. One time, the teachers dressed up in costumes for the school during admin, and the music teacher sang 'I will survive'. It was extremely funny – could you imagine asking one of our teachers to do that!

The school is very large: about 1,500 students attend NPGHS (New Plymouth Girls' High School) and, as the name of the school suggests, all of them are girls. There is also a New Plymouth Boys' High School, which is not far away, but is situated across from a stream and the cemetery so that the girls and boys do not meet too often. Two weeks ago, there was a 'prom[2] night'. That was a dance for both schools, which took place at Boys' High. It was a bit like the dance clubs at home, and I was not too excited about it, but for the students here, it was a real event, because New Plymouth is very rural. It is not a big town, and the boys and girls here are not used to going out as much as young Germans are.

At school, we have to wear uniforms. The colours are dark blue and white. At first, it was hard for me to get used to: Imagine 1,500 girls walking around in the same uniforms – it makes you dizzy[3]! But actually, it is quite

---

[1]**tuition fee** charge for education, teaching [2]**prom** formal dance party for high school students, esp. at the end of an academic year [3]**dizzy** confused, crazy

nice to get up every morning without having to think about what to wear. I'm quite busy in the morning as I have to get up so early to catch my school bus. Classes begin at 8:00 a.m. Sometimes, my host dad takes me to school in his truck. But it is hard to climb out of a truck with the tight long skirt that is part of my school uniform. John (my host dad) always has a good laugh at me when he drops me off. Now you know all about my school here. I hope you are having as much fun as I'm having and I look forward to your next mail.

Cheers, Maria

New Plymouth Girls' High School

NPGHS "is recognised both nationally and beyond New Zealand for providing excellence in education. By offering a wide choice of subjects and by encouraging participation in the extensive range of sporting, cultural and social activities available at the school, the school demonstrates its commitment to developing the potential of each young woman." (from: www.npghs.com) Here is an extract from the school prospectus.

We aim to

- provide a secure environment for students to work and study in, with a sense of WHĀNAU[1] or family and belonging.
- encourage our students to do their best at all they undertake.
- encourage all our students to be involved and have a go at a wide range of sporting, cultural or social activities.
- encourage our students to look beyond themselves – at their world, at other cultures – all the while developing their sense of responsibility, citizenship and cultural awareness.

Boarding

"Scotlands", the school's on-site hostel, provides excellent boarding opportunities for 140 girls.

International Students

The school welcomes applications from international students. They are expected to stay in "Scotlands Hostel". Individual programmes are overseen and set up and ESOL[2] teachers will help with English language as required. Our school has a long-standing tradition of welcoming students from the Pacific Islands, and in recent years has also had students from Japan, Korea, Thailand, and Europe.

---

[1]**whānau** [ˈfanaʊ] the extended family, *here* school community [2]**ESOL E**nglish for **s**peakers of **o**ther **l**anguages

Rotorua Boys' High School

This is the beginning of the RBHS Newsletter from February, 2009 sent to the parents of new students. Read more about the school's aims and expectations.

Dear Parents,

Nga mihi nui ki a koutou me te tangi hoki ki a ratau kua riro atu!

Welcome to the 2009 school year at Rotorua Boys' High School!

I take this opportunity to extend a special welcome to all staff and students who are new to our exciting and successful school. I wish all members of our school the very best for this new school year. [...]

Mr A. C. Grinter, Principal

RBHS – Main building

VISION
To be the outstanding Boys' High School in New Zealand

PRINCIPLES
RBHS provides an environment for boys to mature into outstanding[1] young men to prepare them for the important future role they must play in the community. We will celebrate: 1. Academic excellence; 2. Sporting excellence; 3. Achievements in cultural activities; 4. The development of leadership; 5. The development of citizenship.

VALUES

Students are expected to:

- Be strong of character – *Pūmau*
  Being strong of character means you show respect for both yourself and others, have personal integrity, take responsibility for the consequences of your actions and be a good citizen. Be a good man.
- Demonstrate leadership – *Whakaatu ngārahutanga*
  Leadership can be taught and learned. You will have many opportunities to demonstrate leadership and be a good role model as well as encouraging appropriate behaviour in others. Be a good leader.
- Display commitment – *Ūpoko pakaru*
  Commitment means never giving up just because something is difficult. It encompasses a work ethic, time management and sacrifice in achieving your goals. Be a good worker.
- Take opportunities – *Kapo huanga*
  Taking opportunities is about embracing new challenges. You will be presented with a myriad[2] of opportunities in your time at Rotorua Boys' High School. Enjoy the challenge.
- Strive[3] for excellence – *Hiratanga*
  Striving for excellence means you will always do your best, learn from your mistakes and seek continual improvement. Reach for the stars.

---

[1]**outstanding** excellent [2]**myriad** very many, countless [3]**to strive** to make a great effort

Activities

1. A friend of yours wants to know what school life is like in New Zealand. Sum up in German what you have learned from the texts. — *Mediating*

2. After you have read about the educational and social aims of NPGHS and RBHS, discuss what the principles and aims of your school are or should be. Work in groups to write different statements on this topic. — *School principles*

3. Choose one topic to write an essay about: — *Writing an essay*
   a) Are co-educational schools better than boys- or girls-only schools?
   b) The pros and cons of wearing school uniforms.
   c) Ad astra per aspera – a motto for our school.

4. Surf the Internet to collect more information about both schools. Imagine you want to enrol in one of them. Write a formal letter of application in which you give reasons why you want to attend this school. — *Writing an application letter*

Sports and Leisure Activities

New Zealanders Are People of Action

White water rafting on the Kaituna river, Rotorua

In New Zealand, sport has been referred to as a national religion. This may be true but it is definitely not just 'rugby, racing and beer', although the All Blacks[1] did win the World's Rugby Cup in 1987, and the thoroughbred[2] yearling[3] sales do attract leading world buyers.

It is natural for a New Zealander to lead an active life. From an early age, New Zealanders are encouraged to participate in a variety of team and individual sports. Yachtsmen, canoeists, equestrians, squash and triathlon athletes have gained top international reputations. But at grass root level, the emphasis on all sport in New Zealand is participation.

There is a fine line between sport and leisure activities in New Zealand. With wide open spaces, 'Kiwis' enjoy the outdoor life. Tramping[4] is universally popular, especially in the many National Parks found on both Islands. Mountaineering, cross-country and heli-skiing are only for the more daring. However, there are numerous commercial and club ski-fields available to acquire the necessary skills.

Other favoured activities are wood-chopping and sawing, Highland dancing, athletics and cycling – basically, there is fun for everyone.

The 'Kiwi' typically has an adventurous nature. Perhaps that is why rafting has become so popular. There is certainly enough 'white water' in the rivers of both islands which is graded from 1 to 5 according to the ability (and nerve) needed.

Countless other activities go on around the country, with large numbers of enthusiastic participants. Some examples are surf carnivals, fun runs, and coast to coast triathlons. In short, it can be said that New Zealanders are truly people of action.

---

[1]**All Blacks** nickname of the National Rugby Union team [2]**thoroughbred** a horse that has parents of the same very good breed [3]**yearling** animal between one and two years old [4]**tramping** bushwalking, hiking

Top five sports played by young people (5 – 17 years old)

	1. Sports		2. Active Leisure	
Boys	Rugby Union	24 %	Swimming	27 %
	Soccer	23 %	Cycling	20 %
	Cricket	19 %	Exercising	18 %
	Basketball	11 %	Outdoor games	16 %
	Touch rugby	9 %	Running/jogging	15 %
Girls	Netball	18 %	Swimming	32 %
	Soccer	12 %	Exercising	25 %
	Athletics	10 %	Outdoor games	19 %
	Basketball	8 %	Cycling	17 %
	Tennis	7 %	Walking	17 %

Note:
The percentages are based on young people who are active participants; for example, 23 % of boys who are club members play soccer, the figure for all boys is around 6 %. Similarly 32 % of boys who take part in sport and active leisure with family or friends go swimming, the figure for all boys is around 16 %.

Bungee Jumping

You have probably read and heard the term 'extreme sports' quite often. Activities such as mountain biking, white water rafting, bungee jumping, barefoot skiing, base jumping, kite landboarding, jetboating or skydiving, which attract many enthusiasts and large numbers of spectators, are growing in popularity, especially among young people.

Bungee jumping has a long tradition as a cultural rite of several nations and is still practised today, for example, on the Island of Pentecost in Vanuatu. The word 'bungee' is said to be Kiwi slang for an elastic strap. Commercial bungee jumping began with a New Zealander in 1986, when A. J. Hacket made his first jump from Greenhithe Bridge in Auckland.

Read the blogs in which bungee jumpers – in a very colloquial style – express their feelings right after jumping into the void[1].

"my first jump at twilight in october. people who have been there and done that say 'aye!'"

"my 1st jump last week off this tower. just look to the water"

"aye! cool experience ... incredible!! will probably do australia next"

"aye! did my 3rd jump already from there in June. looking for the next one."

"did it for my girlfriend and it was ... [four-letter word[2]] !!!! awesome!!!!! what a rush!"

"I wish I could do it again!!! and again!!! and again!!!"

"I jumped on three days ago ... my first bungee jump in life! Great! What a feeling!"

"Aye!! Did it in Nov! Now when I have done the highest I can go for the second in South Africa."

"Aye! Still flying. What an experience!!!"

"Oh, I did my first jump in May, I really wanna do it again!"

[1]**void** empty space [2]**four-letter word** offensive word, often consisting of four letters

Extreme sports are fun!

Activities

1. After reading the table on page 80, compare which sports are practised in NZ schools and in your school or area. Is there a sport you would like to be able to do in your school or community? Why?

   Comparing schools in NZ and Germany

2. According to the New Zealand Herald, rugby, cricket, league, soccer, netball, basketball, golf, tennis, motorsport, yachting and racing are among the most popular of New Zealand's sports. Search the web for current information on these disciplines in Aotearoa: www.nzherald.co.nz/sport/news/headlines.cfm?c_id=4.

   Typical NZ sports

3. Find out and explain what these extreme sports are about: mountain biking, white water rafting, bungee jumping, barefoot skiing, base jumping, kite landboarding, jetboating, skydiving.

   Investigating extreme sports

4. Write a blog post about an adventurous experience you have had.

   Writing blogs

Films and Books

King Kong
2005, remake of the 1933 film, produced by NZ film-maker Peter Jackson, stars Naomi Watt

Whale Rider
2003, produced by South Pacific Pictures, NZ's biggest TV production company

The Lord of the Rings
trilogy, 2001–2003, US and NZ-funded, produced in NZ

Once Were Warriors
1994, the film is set in Auckland and was produced in English and Māori versions

The Piano
1993, its music by Michael Nyman became a bestselling soundtrack album

I never knew this about New Zealand

- Middle Earth, Hobbiton, Mount Doom, the Misty Mountains – they all lie in Aotearoa. One of the world's greatest film productions "The Lord of the Rings" (2001–2003) was adapted from Tolkien's books by Oscar-winning producer Peter Jackson and shot in New Zealand's wild and unspoiled landscapes. Of the $560 million spent on the making of the trilogy, much stayed in the country.
- "Whale Rider", the highly praised film about Māori myths and traditions, was produced by Niki Caro in 2002. Her script is based on the 1987 novel by the famous Māori author Witi Ihimaera. The film has won several international awards.
- More must-see films: "The Piano" (1993), written and directed by NZ-born film-maker Jane Campion, the music became a bestselling soundtrack album; and "Once Were Warriors" (1994 by Lee Tamahori of Māori ancestry). This very impressive film tells the story of a poor Māori family living in the slums and battling with alcoholism and violence. The story is based on a book of the same name written by Alan Duff, a former student of the Rotorua Boys' High School.
- Rena Owe who played the protagonist in "Once Were Warriors", Keisha Castle-Hughes (who was the youngest person ever nominated for an Oscar for her role in the "Whale Rider"), Anna Paquin ("The Piano"), Temuera Morrison ("Star Wars"), and Wellington-born Russell Crowe ("Robin Hood") are but a few of the NZ-born actors who have become famous worldwide.

Films Important to New Zealand's Economy

Whether it be Middle-Earth, Narnia or even America's rural heartland in *The Bridge to Terabithia*, New Zealand's ever-versatile[1] landscape has stood in for many places around – and indeed beyond – this world.
But the eeriest[2] of all would have to be Barrow, a remote Alaskan town where the sun doesn't rise for a month during winter, making it the perfect hunting ground for a band of ravenous[3] vampires who ruthlessly[4] prey[5] on the helpless townsfolk in *30 Days of Night*. The film was mostly shot last year at Henderson Valley Studios in Auckland.
Locally produced movies like *Stone's Wedding* and *Black sheep* may be important to the national culture, but international productions like *30 Days of Night* are really what Helen Clark is alluding to when she refers to the importance of film to the New Zealand economy.

---

[1]**versatile** very different [2]**eerie** strange and frightening [3]**ravenous** very hungry [4]**ruthlessly** *gnadenlos* [5]**to prey** to hunt and eat

Whale Rider

"In the old days, the land felt a great emptiness. It was waiting ... waiting to be filled up ... waiting for someone to love it ... waiting for a leader. And he came on the back of a whale ... a man to lead a new people. Our ancestor, Paikea." – These are the film's first magical words, spoken to mystical background music. "Whale Rider" tells the story of Paikea, a Māori girl. Her grandfather Koro is the Chief of their tribe. According to the old traditions, he has to choose a young male to be his successor. None of the boys has the qualities needed though, only Pai has, and so she cannot escape her destiny[1] ...
In the following scene, Pai dares to speak to her tribe for the first time. She is very nervous, but firmly sticks to her mission, says what she has to say, and finally, begins singing their traditional chant.

Keisha Castle-Hughes

- Ladies and gentlemen, please welcome Miss Paikea Apirana.
- Did you know about this?
- She said she had a surprise ... for him.
- (Pai) This speech is a token[2] of my deep love and respect ... for Koro Apirana, my grandfather. My name is Paikea Apirana ...
- Go on, bub[3].
- (Pai) ... and I come from a long line of chiefs, stretching all the way back to Hawaiiki ... where our ancient ones are ... the ones that first heard the land crying and sent a man. His name was also Paikea ... and I am his mo ... most recent descendant. But I was not the leader my grandfather was expecting ... and by being born ... I broke the line back to the ancient ones. It wasn't anybody's fault. It just happened ...
- Who is to blame?
- (Pai) ... but we can learn. And if the knowledge is given to everyone, we can have lots of leaders. And soon, everyone will be strong ... not just the ones that've been chosen. Because sometimes, even if you're the leader and you need to be strong ... you can get tired. Like our ancestor, Paikea, when he was lost at sea ... and he couldn't find the land, and he probably wanted to die. But he knew the ancient ones were there for him ... so he called out to them to lift him up and give him strength. This is his chant. I dedicate[4] it to my grandfather.

[1]**destiny** fate [2]**token** *here* sign, symbol [3]**bub** *infml.* word usually used to address a man [4]**to dedicate** to state that something is done in order to show respect to a person

Activities

1. What strength of character does Paikea reveal in this scene? Discuss.

Comprehension

2. Work in pairs. Decide which NZ film or actor you are most interested in. Prepare a multimedia presentation about your choice. As a class, decide which film you want to watch. After viewing it, discuss it together.

Giving a multimedia presentation

3. One of the world's greatest literary figures is Wellington-born short-story writer Katherine Mansfield. Make a poster about her life and work, about Witi Ihimaera and a third New Zealand author of your choice.

Making a poster

The 3-D science fiction film "Avatar" (2009) was also shot in NZ.

Politics and People

How Government Works

Queen Elizabeth II

Governor-General Anand Satyanand

New Zealand is an independent parliamentary, constitutional democracy within the British Commonwealth. Read this short introduction to New Zealand's political system.

The Sovereign[1], or the de facto Head of State is Queen Elizabeth II, Queen of New Zealand, who is represented in New Zealand by the Governor-General. Parliament consists of the Sovereign and the House of Representatives, which is the sole chamber of legislature in New Zealand. Parliament is elected every three years by Mixed Member Proportional Representation (MMP) – a voting system introduced in 1993 as a result of two referenda. In line with this system, all New Zealanders over the age of 18 have the right to vote. There are 120 Members of Parliament, some of whom represent a geographical electorate[2], while others enter Parliament as a party representative. The first Parliament elected under MMP saw a significant increase in the representation of Māori, ethnic minorities and women. Of the 120 MPs in the current Parliament, 37 are women, 16 are Māori, four are Pacific Islanders and one is Chinese-born. Parliament sits in Wellington, the capital city of New Zealand. The Prime Minister is Head of Government, supported by a Cabinet of Ministers chosen from the elected Members of Parliament. Government policy is implemented[3] by 38 public service departments.

---

[1]**sovereign** a king or queen [2]**electorate** all the people in a particular area that have the right to vote [3]**to implement** to put into action, to carry out

Former Governor-General Dame Silvia Cartwright

I never knew this about New Zealand

- The Governor-General is an essential part of Parliament and has a formal role. This includes agreeing to bills passed in the House of Representatives so that they become Acts of Parliament.
- After a general election, the Governor-General opens Parliament by delivering the speech from the Throne. The speech from the Throne sets out the Government's intentions for the coming term of Parliament. The Governor-General also brings a parliamentary term to an end. This is known as 'dissolution'. Nevertheless, the Governor-General has no part in the daily activities of the House of Representatives.
- The current Governor-General is Anand Satyanand, who was born to an Indo-Fijian family. He was sworn in on 23 August, 2006. His predecessor in office was Dame Silvia Cartwright. Her term as Governor-General was from 2001 to 2006. In those years, for the first (and so far only) time in a Commonwealth country, the Monarch (Elizabeth II), Governor-General (Dame S. Cartwright), Chief Justice (Dame S. Elias) and Prime Minister (H. Clark) were all female.

Central Government – Prime Ministers

New Zealand's Prime Minister John Key (National Party) was elected during the November 2008 General Election. He heads the Central Government which he has said "will be focused on growth to deliver prosperity for all New Zealanders". Before him, Helen Clark, the Labour Party's longest serving woman member among current MPs, served as the 37th Prime Minister in three successive terms from 1999 to 2008. She ranks among the most powerful women of the world. Read an extract from an interview with Helen Clark in summer 2007.

Prime Minister John Key

Former Prime Minister Helen Clark

> "New Zealand is not a sleepy hollow[1], not a backwater. It's a sexy and modern advanced nation. It's a great place to do business with, it's a great place to migrate to and live in, and on the international scene, it stands for something which is good and decent[2]. We need to update the image so that New Zealand is not just beautiful, but also creative, innovative, safe, desirable[3]. That's it in a nutshell." (Helen Clark)

NZ Inspired: What are the top three items on your domestic[4] agenda?
HC: The top three items will be strengthening the economy, then social policy and Kiwi identity. Firstly, the economy: I think that anyone who looked at it objectively would say that the New Zealand economy has done incredibly well. The economy has become more sophisticated[5] and is able to export more goods and services of a higher value. So where the high dollar hasn't been easy for exporters, nonetheless because we have moved up the value chain and are in a position to make more prices, rather than just take them, we've done quite well. In the end, a strong economy isn't enough in itself. It's there so that you can guarantee the best possible life for people. We are being very proactive on social policy in terms of older people, families, and very proactive in job creation. We do have unemployment lower than Britain, and we've done quite a lot on housing. A lot of things have changed: four weeks annual holiday, paid parental leave[6], and, probably most helpful for working parents, a move to pay for 20 hours free early childhood education (per week). Then there's been the big area of debate that surrounds New Zealand identity: Who are we? What do we represent? How do we express it in our foreign policy? We're looking at that through the creative arts, the support we give our sports people, through what we stand for at home in terms of reconciliation[7] under the Treaty of Waitangi.

---

[1] **sleepy hollow** *here* poor and undeveloped village or town [2] **decent** of good quality [3] **desirable** worth having or doing [4] **domestic** *here* inland [5] **sophisticated** *here* well developed, very advanced [6] **parental leave** time that a parent is allowed to spend away from work with his or her baby [7] **reconciliation** process of trusting and becoming friendly with each other again after a time of quarrelling

Main parties in NZ:

National Party
centre-right; conservative

Labour Party
centre-left; progressive

Green Party
left-wing; promotes environmental ideas

Māori Party
promotes Māori interests

ACT Party
liberal; promotes free market and low taxation

United Future Party
centre-right; strongly Christian

Women play an important role

- New Zealand was the first country in the world to introduce women's right to vote in general elections in 1893. In 1919, women won the right to stand in general elections when the Women's Parliamentary Rights Act was passed. However, none of the four women who stood in the 1919 election were elected.
- Just three years later, in 1922, the New Zealand Federation of University Women was established to provide a contact network for women graduates, encourage ongoing education, and support research through grants to female students.
- The first woman MP, Elizabeth McCombs, was elected in the by-election for Lyttelton[1] in 1933.
- In the 1970s, PACIFICA, a non-party political organisation of Pacific women, was established in Auckland. Also, the first New Zealand woman ambassador – Barbara Angus – was appointed to the Philippines.
- The Ministry of Women's Affairs was established in 1984 to provide policy advice and information on women throughout government sectors and to the general public. *Te Ohu Whakatupu* is the Māori Women's Policy Unit within the Ministry. Secretary of Women's Affairs, Katherine O'Regan, was the first woman to head a government department.
- In 1996, in the first General Election held under the Mixed Member Proportional Representation Electoral System, 36 women MPs were elected, making up 30 percent.
- In 2004, the Government launched an Action Plan for New Zealand Women which was focused on three key areas: improving the economic independence of women; achieving greater work-life balance for families; and improving the well-being and quality of life of New Zealand women. Margaret Wilson became New Zealand's first woman Speaker of the House of Representatives in 2005.

[1] **Lyttelton** little town close to Christchurch (South Island)

Activities

Comprehension
1. How is the New Zealand Parliament elected?

Giving a summary
2. Sum up what you have learned from this chapter about New Zealand's political system, and compare it to the British political system.

Translating into German
3. Translate Helen Clark's answer in the interview (p. 85) into German.

Discussing women's role in NZ and in Germany
4. How many women have a seat in New Zealand's parliament? Compare this to the number of female MPs in the German Bundestag. Do you think women play a big part in the politics of both countries? Discuss.

Giving a presentation
5. Prepare a presentation on women in Aotearoa. Use the website www.stats.govt.nz. and the information given above.

Not Just Sheep and Wool

Innovative Economy

With five million cattle and almost 40 million sheep (2002), New Zealand has a world-wide reputation as an efficient and innovative producer of agricultural products. Almost half of the nation's export earnings are derived from farming. However, the country also has strong secondary and tertiary industries. It has abundant sources of water, which can be harnessed for hydro-powered electricity, and geothermal power offers an interesting alternative energy source. In addition, exciting hydrocarbon finds have given hope for a future not totally reliant on the importing of oil. Natural gas and oil are already being successfully drilled. Based on these resources, the country has resisted the need for nuclear powered generators, and in fact, has the aim of generating 90 per cent of its electricity from renewable sources by 2025.
Read two extracts from articles in *The New Zealander*.

Auckland, North Island – largest city and centre of the NZ economy

Harvesting power from the skies

But now we are getting ready to dam the skies. Two of the proposed new wind farm schemes – Project Hayes in Central Otago and Port Waktato, south of Auckland – are planned to have an even greater megawatt output than a hydro dam like Benmore or Clyde. Meridian Energy's $2 billion Project Hayes wind farm in the Lammermoor Range, for example involves 1,786 turbines each 160 m high – about the height of a 50-storey building – with a potential total output of 630 MW. By comparison, Benmore Dam, the largest power station on the Waitaki, is rated at 540 MW. All of a sudden, like Germany, Denmark, the USA and many others, we are looking toward a new era of grand energy schemes where a fifth to a quarter of our electricity needs will be met by harnessing the wind. And this is a revolution that may trickle down all the way to the average householder. So as with hydro, New Zealand is a lucky country.

Hydroelectric dam

Electric cars set for Kiwi trials next year

Electric cars are to be tried on New Zealand roads next year. The Mitsubishi Innovative Electric Vehicle – known as the MIEV – features an energy-efficient electric motor powered by recyclable lithium-ion batteries. It will be brought to New Zealand in conjunction with Meridian Energy, and will be used for trial and promotional purposes when it arrives early next year. The car produces no emissions and fits with the Government's aim to have a largely electric-fuelled fleet by 2050. [...] New Zealand will be one of the first countries in the world to host the car, despite overwhelming international demand.

Electric car

New Zealand's Import and Export

Principal Sources of Imports*		Principal Export Markets*	
Australia	6,844.0	Australia	5,130.0
USA	5,135.0	USA	3,636.0
Japan	3,474.0	Japan	3,343.0
China	1,631.0	UK	1,356.0
Germany	1,183.0	Rep. of Korea	1,163.0
UK	1,161.0	China	725.0

* For year ended June 2000 in million NZ $

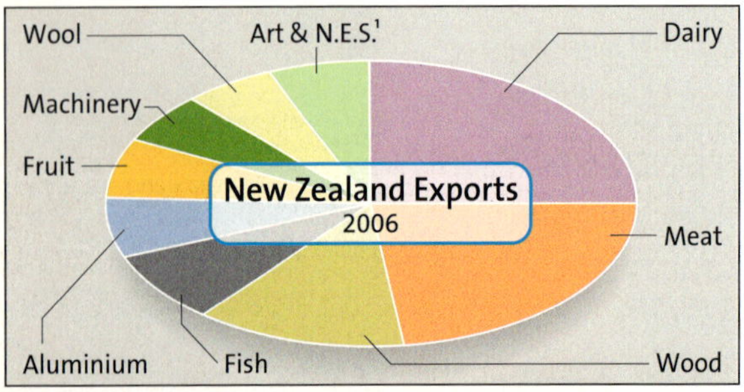

Agrodome Rotorua

I never knew this about New Zealand

- There were roughly 39.2 million sheep in New Zealand as of 30 June 2002, the lowest recorded level since 1955. There has been a steady decline in sheep numbers since 1982, when the national flock peaked at 70.3 million sheep. The country is one of the world's largest exporters of wool, and accounts for a quarter of the world's international dairy trade (notably butter, cheese and milk powder).
- Horticulture also contributes significantly to the economy. New Zealand apples and kiwifruit are exported worldwide. New Zealand white wines have also won awards in several countries.
- Additionally, New Zealand has many mineral resources, chiefly natural gas, oil and coal, which provide domestic and industrial fuel. Other resource-based industries include forestry and forest products, fisheries, tanneries[2], cement works, fertilizer factories and glasswork. Heavy industries include steel works, aluminium smelters and oil refineries.
- Main imports include oil products, sugar, clothing and electronic goods.

[1] **N.E.S.** goods which are **n**ot **e**lsewhere **s**pecified [2] **tannery** a place where animal skin is made into leather

Activities

Comprehension

1. What are New Zealand's main sources of energy?

Interpreting statistics

2. What does the import-export table tell you about New Zealand's trade relations?

Giving a presentation

3. Surf the web for more information on New Zealand's agriculture and industry, and then prepare a presentation on this topic.

New Zealand's Nature – Beauty and Beast

New Zealand's Hazards

Te Puia (above) and Hell's Gate (below), both Rotorua, North Island

Returning from a visit to Hell's Gate thermal park in Rotorua in 1934, George Bernard Shaw is said to have remarked, "I was pleased to get so close to Hades and be able to return."
Indeed, for such a small country, New Zealand certainly has many natural hazards. Some are related to the weather – flooding, drought, heavy snowfalls, severe hailstorms[1], fog and high winds. Others are caused by land surface instability – e. g. coastal erosion, avalanches[2] and landslides.
Perhaps the most fearsome natural hazards of all, however, result from enormous earth-forming forces deep within the earth – e. g. volcanoes (mainly on the North Island), earthquakes and tsunamis. One of the reasons for this instability is that the isles of New Zealand are located right on top of two separate and unstable sections of the earth's crust called the Indo-Australian Plate and the Pacific Plate. Read more about the most dangerous natural hazards in New Zealand in the text below.

- As New Zealand's economy is based on agriculture, its agriculture relies on stable soil, regular sunshine and rainfall. However, some of New Zealand's most productive farmland is regularly threatened by **drought** and **flood**. Because many settlements are located near river mouths and most New Zealanders live or work in intensively farmed, lowland areas, **flooding** is this country's most common natural hazard.
- Many of New Zealand's vital road, rail, air and sea links are regularly broken by climatic hazards such as flooding, heavy **snowfalls**, high **winds**, **fog** and **ice** and land instability hazards like **landslides**.
- New Zealand's population is distributed unevenly across the country. Most people live in towns and cities. Auckland, the largest population and industrial centre is sited on a major volcanic field. Wellington, the country's capital and administrative centre, is criss-crossed with fault lines and a major **earthquake** could strike at any time.
- There has been an enormous investment in horticulture in the Bay of Plenty on the east coast of the North Island. However, this region is vulnerable to damage from tropical **cyclones** and easterly **storms**. In addition to that, there is the threat of **tsunamis** caused by off-shore **earthquakes** or large volcanic **eruptions** from White Island.
- New Zealand's largest exotic forests, many hydro-dams and a number of important tourist centres are situated on the plateau of the central North Island where **volcanic hazards** are a problem.
- An increasing number of people are flocking to the mountains each winter. **Avalanches** are a hazard in mountain areas, and on the North Island ski fields, there is always the possibility of **volcanic eruptions**.

Arid land near Paradise, a rural community in the Otago region, South Island

---

[1]**hailstorm** storm with frozen raindrops [2]**avalanche** a large mass of snow suddenly sliding down the side of a mountain

New Zealand's Beautiful Landscapes

Read the following extracts from a selection of articles about New Zealand's beautiful and hazardous, but also endangered, landscapes.

Queenstown, South Island (above) and nearby Arthur's Point (below)

A land full of natural beauty

New Zealand's treasure is its landscape. Within these small islands of the southern Pacific Ocean are scenic delights comparable to any in the world – the massive snow-capped peaks of the Southern Alps, with Mt. Cook as the highest peak in the country (3,754 m), or the symmetrical volcanic cones of the Central Plateau, the giant Kauris[1] of Waipoua Forest or the dense rainforest of Westland, the arid highcountry tussockland[2] of the McKenzie Basin or the rolling green pastures of Taranaki, the secluded golden bays of Abel Tasman National Park or the broad 90 Mile Beach of North Cape. The variety is unending – lakes and rivers, fiords and farmlands, all within easy reach of each other.

The absence of predators enabled several species of giant flightless birds to graze New Zealand's forest and pastures before the arrival of man. Only the huge eagle and one species of *moa*[3] remained when the Polynesian hunters arrived. Luckily our national symbol, the Kiwi, still survives, though being a shy nocturnal forest dweller, you will probably only see him in a zoo.

Tongariro National Park

The Volcanic Plateau was home to the most sinister[4] of *The Lord of the Rings* locales: Mordor, the stronghold of the dark Lord Sauron. Mordor is a great volcanic plateau filled with geologic wonders known as Gorgoroth. Much of Frodo and Sam's[5] journey into the land of Sauron was filmed on and around the Volcanic Plateau in the Tongariro National Park. The area has jagged[6] volcanic rock formations and eerie barren landscapes were ideally suited to Mordor's hissing[7] wasteland.

Climbers can trek to the summit of Mt Ngauruhoe. A poled route leads from the Mangatepopo road end (this can also be done as part of the Tongariro Crossing if you really want to immerse yourself in Mordor). At the saddle between Ngauruhoe and Tongariro, the route is not marked. Be aware of the falling rocks dislodged by other climbers. Avoid entering the inner crater area, where volcanic fumaroles[8] may emit overpowering gases. The climb should not be undertaken in winter without mountaineering experience and equipment. Icy slopes can make this climb extremely hazardous.

Subtropical rainforest on the Peninsula Coromandel, North Island

[1] **Kauri** type of tree found only in NZ [2] **tussockland** grassland [3] **moa** extinct, flightless bird [4] **sinister** dark, dangerous [5] **Mordor/Sauron/Frodo/Sam** names invented by J. R. R. Tolkien [6] **jagged** having a rough or pointed surface [7] **hissing** making strange, frightening sounds [8] **fumarole** an opening emitting gas or steam

Shrinking NZ glaciers are smallest since records began

Most of New Zealand's glaciers are now the smallest they have been since records began – and they continue to shrink at a rapid rate. The National Institute of Water and Atmospheric Research, which made the discovery, said global warming was the main culprit[1]. Between April last year and March this year, glaciers in the Southern Alps lost about 2.2 billion tons of permanent ice. It is the fourth highest annual loss since monitoring began 32 years ago. The total ice for the glaciers now comprises an estimated 44.9 cubic kilometres – the lowest on record. The volume of ice dropped by 50 per cent during the last century.

Fox Glacier, on the West Coast of the South Island

Iron like Zion

Iron Gates Gorge[2] is a narrow chasm[3] where the Oroua River squeezes between the walls of sheer sided cliffs as it leaves behind its remote backcountry headwaters and spills into farmland on its way to the sea. Its name reflects the barrier presented by the narrow gorge that guards the entrance to the valley. Located about 90 minutes from the road end, the Iron Gates Gorge provides a comfortable day walk for those wanting to enjoy a mix of easy bush and river travel a little more than an hour from Palmerston North. Not only does the walk offer a mix of terrain, it also provides a true wilderness experience as, once the Oroua River valley is reached, all that can be seen are the high peaks and forest that enclose the valley, despite being only a short distance from the car park and farmland. The track to the gorge leaves from the car park at the end of Peterson's Road, where on fine days, there are sweeping[4] views across to Mt Taranaki and the volcanoes of the central plateau.

Road from Christchurch to Hokitika, South Island

"Split Apple Rock", Abel Tasman National Park

[1]**culprit** *fml.* person or thing responsible for causing something bad [2]**gorge** deep, narrow valley with steep sides [3]**chasm** very deep space between two rocks [4]**sweeping** *here* wide, far-reaching

Activities

1. Explain what the hazards mentioned on page 89 mean. Are they a danger to Germany or Europe, too? Discuss. — *Explaining and discussing*

2. Sum up what the pictures and texts tell you about Aotearoa's landscapes. — *Giving a summary*

3. Make an imaginary trip to New Zealand and find these places on a large-scale map of the country: North Island, South Island, White Island, Rotorua, Taranaki, the Southern Alps, Mount Egmont, Mount Cook, Mount Ngauruhoe, Abel Tasman NP, Tongariro NP. Working in groups, search the web for more information about these and other sights, then make an illustrated map of New Zealand. — *Making a poster*

The Top Ten Eco-Experiences in New Zealand

Mount Ruhapehu, New Zealand's highest volcano, North Island

Mount Cook, or Aoraki, New Zealand's highest mountain, South Island

Kaikoura – Whale Watching

Backpackers' paradise in Anakiwa, North Island

- **Lake Dunstan.** Join an informative, non-impact[1], personalised boat tour of the Bendigo wetlands and appreciate the beauty of the natural ecosystem on the edge of this Central Otago lake.
- **Royal Albatross Centre, Otago Peninsula.** Taiaroa Head is the site of the only mainland breeding colony of this albatross in the world.
- **Penguin Place, Otago Peninsula.** Hide in the hills and watch yellow-eyed penguins as they go about their fascinating lives in this conservation reserve near Dunedin.
- **Milford Sound.** The Milford Deep Underwater Observatory is situated in the middle of Piopiotahi Marine Reserve in Fiordland. It lets you view a completely natural and unaffected marine community – without getting wet.
- **Kapiti Island.** It's easy to arrange a landing permit and transport from Wellington for this internationally-famed nature reserve protecting some of the world's most endangered birds.
- **Cape Kidnapper's Gannet[2] Reserve.** This Hawke's Bay site contains the largest and most accessible mainland gannet colony in the world.
- **Whale Watching in Kaikoura.** Go by boat or air, all year round. You can also experience seal swimming with a land-based or boat-based guided seal snorkeling tour.
- **Nugget Point.** At this stunning and accessible part of the coastal Southland, visitors can view three penguin species, Kooker's sea lions, Hector's dolphins, elephant seals and New Zealand fur seals.
- **The White Heron[3] Sanctuary.** Whataroa on the South Island's West Coast is the only nesting colony of the white heron, or *kotuku,* in NZ.
- **Tiritiri Matangi Island.** This island in Auckland's Hauraki Gulf is one of New Zealand's most important and exciting conservation projects. It is home to many rare native birds, including the *takahe*[4] – and the little spotted kiwi.

---

[1]**non-impact** not affecting nature in a negative way [2]**gannet** large seabird living on cliffs [3]**heron** *Reiher* [4]**takahe** flightless, green and blue bird with short legs (see photo)

Takahe

Activities

1. These are the top ten eco-experiences which are recommended in a magazine. On your map, find where they are located.
2. Discuss and decide which of them you would like to visit. Give reasons why you have chosen this place in New Zealand.

Acknowledgements

Texts

National Youth Week, www.youthweek.com (12.05.2009)
Ahmed Fahour: "A land where all the kids can play", in: *Herald Sun*, April 15, 2008
Penelope Debelle: "Slaying the hackers", in: *The Age*, April 15, 2008
Andrew Prentice: "The day the city came out to say thanks", in: *Manly Daily*, September 16, 2008
Mike Rawlinson: "You don't have to live in Melbourne", in: *Herald Sun*, September 15, 2008
Miawling Lam: "Ur kid's L8 4 school", in: *The Sunday Telegraph*, September 21, 2008
Andrew Stevenson: "Postgraduate Education – All abroad", in: *Herald Sun*, September 21, 2008
Karen Collier: "Their goes you're grammar", in: *Herald Sun*, October 2, 2008
Aboriginal Art, from: Discover the Blue Mountains & Central West, September 2008
Aboriginal Music, from: www.yothuyindi.com (12.05.2009)
Australian Government Culture Portal: Brett Whiteley, http://www.cultureandrecreation.gov.au/articles/brettwhiteley (12.05.2009)
Melina Marchetta: *Finnikin of the Rock*, Penguin Australia, Melbourne 2008
Baz Luhrmann: Australia, from: www.australiamovie.net (12.05.2009), adapted
"Neighbours" – An Australian TV Soap, http://neighbours.com.au (12.05.2009)
Peter Jensen: "What Place Multiculturalism?", in: Peter Goldsworthy (ed.): *True Blue? On Being Australian*, Allen & Unwin, Sydney 2008, pp. 49/50
Ouyang Yu: "Far and Near", in: Peter Goldsworthy (ed.): *True Blue? On Being Australian*, Allen & Unwin, Sydney 2008, p. 49
Tim Winton: "Neighbours", in: Mary Lord: *Best Australian Short Stories*, Penguin Australia, Melbourne 1991, pp. 299–302
E. Himmelreich: "City Welcomes New Citizens", in: *Colac Extra*, September 25, 2008
N.N.: "Australia and Me", interview with Stephen O'Grady, in: *Irish Echo*, September 10–23, 2008
Anni Radle (Melbourne)/Bruno Schwaerzler (Melbourne): Autobiographical letters
Citizenship Testing, from: www.citizenship.gov.au/test/about.htm (adapted)
Shannon Kilgariff (Adelaide): "School of the Air" (letter)
"The Rainbow Snake", retold by form 5 and 6 students of Jessie Younghusband School, Chichester, UK
Jane Harrison: *Stolen*, Langenscheidt, München 2005
Burnum Burnum: "The Burnum Burnum Declaration", in: A. Heiss and P. Minter (eds.): *The Macquarie Pen Anthology of Aboriginal Literature*, Allen & Unwin, Sydney 2008, pp. 124/125
Kevin Rudd: "I move ...", in: *The Sydney Morning Herald*, February 13, 2007

Oodgeroo Noonuccal: "I Am Proud", in: *My People: A Kath Walker Collection*, Jacaranda Press, Queensland 1990

Australian Government: "Becoming an Australian Citizen", 2007, www.ag.gov.au (12.05.2009)

"Australia – Neither Down nor Under", from: www.economywatch.com/world_economy/australia (12.05.2009)

"Parihaka – A Symbol of Protest", from: *Taranaki 2000*, supplement to the *Daily News*, March 30, 1999

"Feel the spirit – Manaakitanga", from: Rotorua Visitor Guide, 2001

"Leaders get experience", in: *The Dominion Post*, March 7, 2007

"tamariki on tv", in: *New Zealand Inspired. Southern Summer 2007*, p. 13

"Kiwis one short in medal hunt", in: *The New Zealander*, September 24, 2008

"Māori heritage in Great Britain", in: *New Zealand Inspired. Southern Summer 2007*, p. 12

Maria Rogahn (Halle/Saale): A High School Year in Aotearoa

"New Zealanders Are People of Action", from: *New Zealand PANORAMA*, Kowhai Publishing, Auckland (adapted)

Stephen Jewell: "Blood Money", in: *New Zealand Inspired. Southern Summer 2007*, pp. 91

"Whale Rider" dialogue transcript, www.script-o-rama.com (12.05.2009)

"How Government Works", from: *New Zealand in Outline*, March 2001

Mary Fenwick: Interview with Helen Clark, in: *New Zealand Inspired. Southern Summer 2007*, p. 23/24

"Harvesting power from the skies"/"Electric cars set for Kiwi trials next year", from: *The New Zealander*, September 24, 2008

"A land full of natural beauty", from: *New Zealand PANORAMA*, Kowhai Publishing, Auckland (adapted)

"Tongariro National Park", from: National Park Village brochure

"Shrinking NZ glaciers are smallest since records began", from: *The New Zealander*, September 24, 2008

"Iron like Zion", from Wilderness. *New Zealand's Magazine of the Outdoors*, March 2009, p. 60

Illustrations

Rainer Berthelmann, Halle: p. 6 top/centre, p. 6/7, p. 8, p. 10 (7 pictures), p. 12, p. 13, p. 14 top, p. 17, p. 18, p. 20, p. 21, p. 22 centre (2 pictures) and bottom, p. 24, p. 25 bottom, p. 27 bottom, p. 28 top, p. 32 bottom, p. 33, p. 35, p. 36, p. 37, p. 38, p. 41 centre, p. 42 bottom, p. 44, p. 46, p. 47 bottom, p. 48, p. 50 (6 pictures), p. 51, p. 52 bottom, p. 59 (7 pictures), p. 64 centre top, p. 67 bottom (2 pictures), Melanie Engelhardt, Halle: p. 6 bottom, p. 59 top centre, p. 64 top; Harald Kupfer, Hummelshain: p. 10 (Kookaburra, Daintree), p. 26 centre, p. 41 top/bottom, p. 42 top, p. 50 bottom left, p. 64 bottom (2 pictures); © TED MEAD/WWI/Still Pictures: p. 10 bottom right; © Rhiana Chan: p. 15 top; © Tom Stanford: p. 15 bottom; © www.manlydaily.com.au: p. 19; picture-alliance/dpa: p. 22 top, p. 30 bottom, p. 60; REUTERS/STR New: p. 25 top; © Bula'bula Arts 2004: p. 25 centre; © National Bank of Australia: p. 26 top; Matthias Berghahn/Verlagsarchiv Schöningh: p. 26 bottom; © Annabelle_82: p. 27 top; © Penguin Books Australia: p. 28 bottom; defd: p. 29, p. 83; © www.backpackerking.com.au: p. 30 top; © Diane Glover: p. 31; Photo: Ken Robertson: p. 32 top; © www.irishecho.com.au: p. 40; Image courtesy Zhengming Wan, MODIS Land Surface Temperature Group, Institute for Computational Earth System Science, University of California, Santa Barbara: p. 52 top; © Jessie Younghusband School, Chichester: p. 53; © www.aboriginalartstore.com.au: p. 54, p. 55 right (4 illustrations); National Maritime Museum, Greenwich, UK: p. 56 bottom; © Brian Jenkins: p. 57; National Archives of Australia: p. 58; © Curriculum Corporation and National Archives of Australia, 2007-09: p. 61; action press/REX FEATURES LTD.: p. 62 top; REUTERS/Ho New: p. 62 bottom; © www.alp.org.au: p. 63 top; © www.liberal. org.au: p. 63 centre; © www.nationals. org. au: p. 63 bottom; Stephan Essendorfer (Dunedin, NZ): p. 66 top left, p. 87 top/centre, p. 92 (2 pictures); Jana Kohl (Oxford, UK): p. 66 top right/bottom left, p. 72 left (2 pictures), p. 80 (2 pictures), p. 89 centre (2 pictures) and bottom, p. 90 top/centre, p. 91 top/centre, p. 92 top; Verena Körner, Usingen: p. 66 centre left/bottom right, p. 71 bottom, p. 89 top, p. 91 bottom, p. 92 centre; © Bachmann/F1 online: p. 66 centre right; Birgit Ziesemann (Auckland, NZ): p. 67 top; © ullstein bild - imagestate: p. 67 bottom right; Kimbell Art Museum, Fort Worth, Texas: p. 68; Jenny Ellis/Kim Jennings, New Plymouth Girls' High School, NZ: p. 69; Lisa Becker, Usingen: p. 71 top, p. 81 (3 pictures), p. 90 bottom; © www.rotoruanz.com: p. 74 top; © www.auckland.ac.nz: p. 74 centre; © 2007 New Zealand Inspired: p. 74 bottom; © 2009 Museum of Archaeology & Anthropology, Cambridge: p. 75 bottom; Jenny Ellis/Kim Jennings, New Plymouth Girls' High School, NZ: p. 76 (2 pictures), p. 77 (3 pictures); © Rotorua Boys' High School, NZ: p. 78 top; Chris Grinter/Colleen Crew, Rotorua Boys' High School, NZ: p. 78 bottom, p. 79, p. 88 (2 pictures); Official Photographic Portrait of Her Majesty The Queen, http://www.canadianheritage.gc.ca: p. 84 top; © www.unitedway.org.nz: p. 84 centre; Ministry for Culture and Heritage, www.nzhistory.net. nz: p. 84 bottom; Photo by Ross Setford/NZPA: p. 85 top; © www.undp.org: p. 85 bottom; © www.national.org.nz: p. 86 top; © http://labourparty.org.nz: p. 86 centre top; © www.greens.org.nz: p. 86 centre bottom; © www.maoriparty.org: p. 86 bottom; picturealliance/landov: p. 87 bottom; Photography: Peter Moore: p. 92 bottom; other illustrations: Verlagsarchiv Schöningh